Getting Started with Computing Concepts

**Prentice Hall
Information Technology**

Prentice
Hall

Prentice Hall
*Upper Saddle River,
New Jersey 07458*

Acquisitions Editor: Jodi McPherson
Editor-in-Chief: Natalie Anderson
Project Manager (Editorial): Eileen Clark
Editorial Assistant: Jodi Bolognese
Senior Marketing Manager: Emily Knight
Marketing Assistant: Scott Patterson
Production, Manager (Production): Gail Steier de Acevedo
Project Manager (Production): Lynne Breitfeller
Associate Director, Manufacturing: Vincent Scelta
Manufacturing Buyer: Lynne Breitfeller
Design Manager: Maria Lange
Designer: Chris Kossa
Composition: Digital Content Factory
Printer/Binder: Banta, Menasha

Pearson Education LTD.
Pearson Education Australia PTY, Limited
Pearson Education Singapore, Pte. Ltd
Pearson Education North Asia Ltd
Pearson Education, Canada, Ltd
Pearson Educación de Mexico, S.A. de C.V.
Pearson Education-Japan
Pearson Education Malaysia, Pte. Ltd

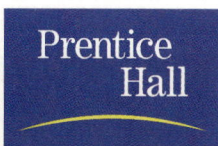

Prentice
Hall

10 9 8 7 6 5 4 3 2
ISBN 0-13-141135-7

Contents

Basic Computer Concepts

- **Computers Defined**
- **Common Applications**

OBJECTIVES: When you have finished this chapter, you will be able to define what a computer is and understand what a computer is used for.

Computers Defined

What Is a Computer?

At its most basic, a computer is a machine that you use to run programs to produce a result or accomplish a task.

To use a computer, you need to input data, which includes numbers, dates, words, sentences, images, and so on. A program (also known as an application) manipulates this data to create a final result. For example, words make up a document; images, words, and sounds make up a Web site, and so on.

Common Applications

The following are just a few examples of where and how computers are used.

Home

- Surf the Internet for movie theatre times

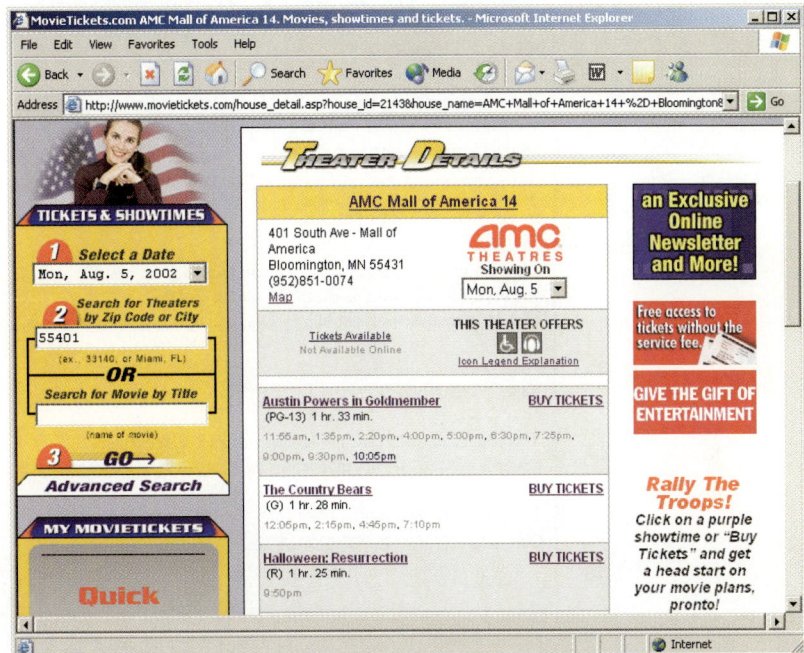

- Write and print a school project

- Send and receive e-mail

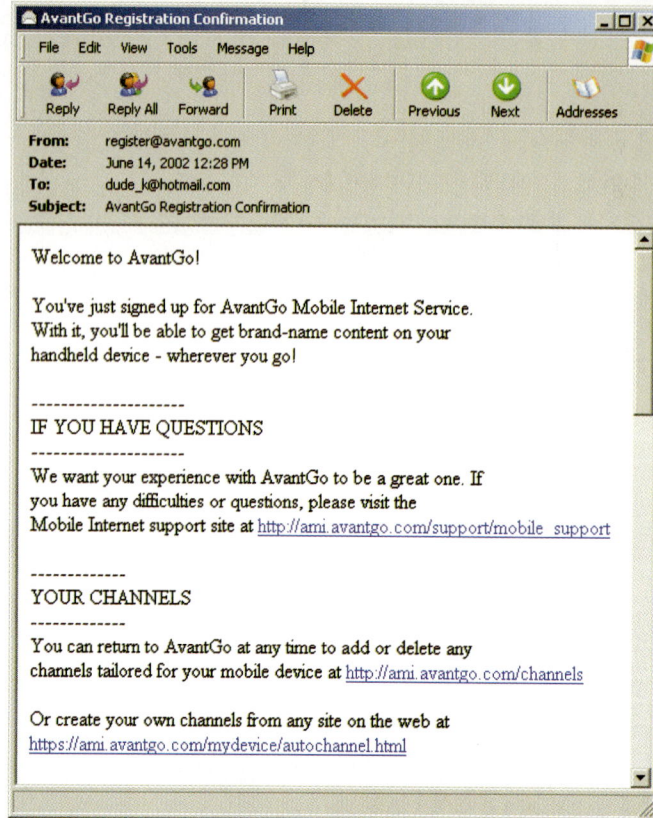

Business

- Create and distribute business reports
- Send and receive business e-mail
- Create, update, and access product catalogue databases

- Access Internet services

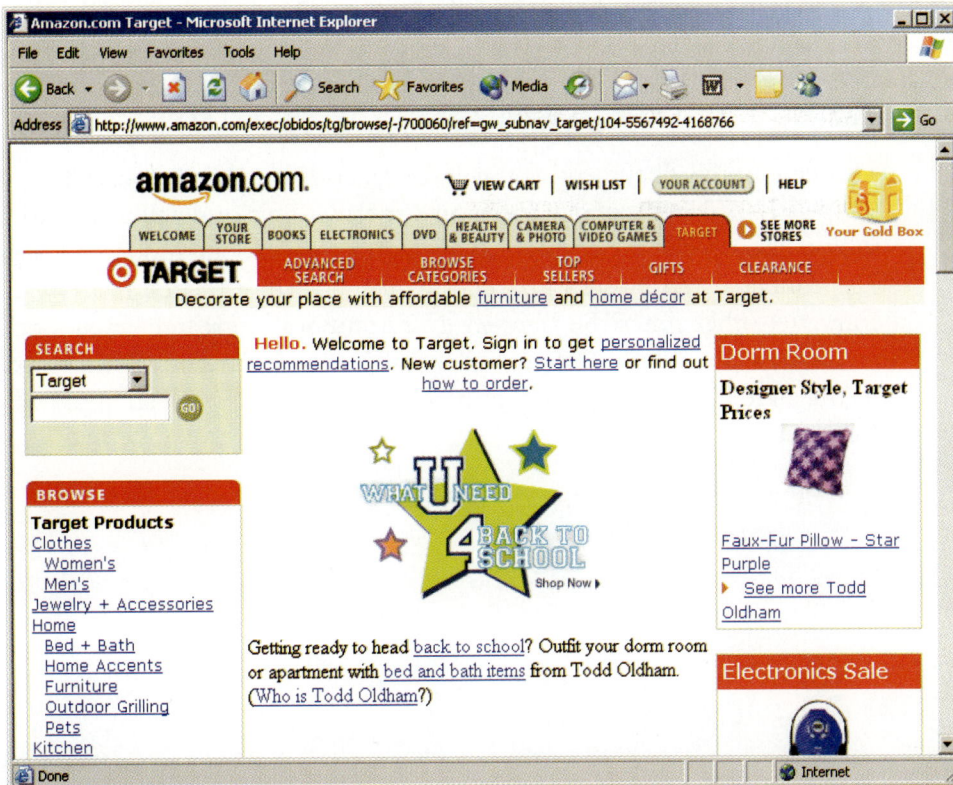

Industry

- Work with CAD/CAM (computer assisted drawing/computer assisted machining) programs

- Use specially created Web sites for business-to-business (B2B) transactions

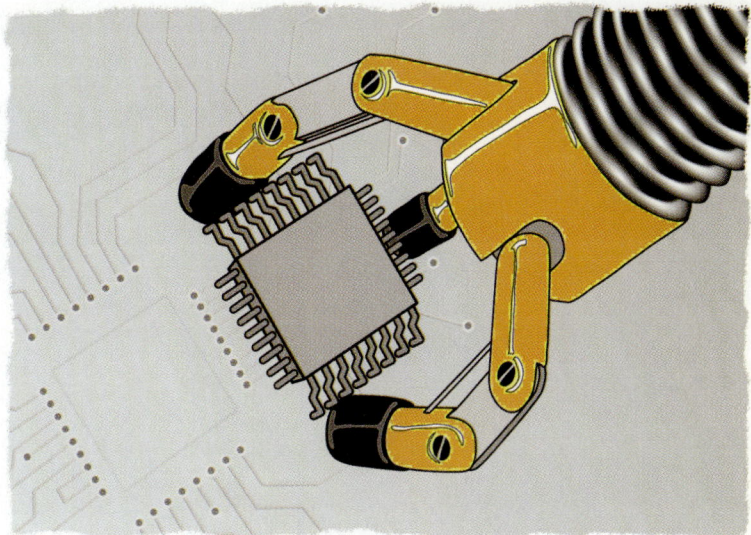

COMPUTE THIS: Expand Your Computer Knowledge

Throughout this document, you will see sections like this one, called *Compute This*. These sections focus on a specific topic or detail related to the subject discussed in the chapter in which they appear. Sometimes the *Compute This* contains step-by-step instructions to perform a related task on your compute; other times the *Compute This* examines in greater detail a point mentioned previously. But regardless of how it is presented, these extra sections are designed to give you practical knowledge you can apply when you use your computer.

Hardware

- **Types of Computers**
- **What Is Hardware?**
- **Microcomputer Hardware Components**

OBJECTIVES: When you have finished this chapter, you will be able to define the main types of computers. You will have learned what hardware is and be able to describe the many kinds of hardware that can exist in and outside of a computer.

Types of Computers

There are many types of computers, but in general, they can be divided into two groups: supercomputers/mainframes, and microcomputers.

Supercomputers and Mainframes

A **supercomputer** is a large, extremely powerful computer. It is usually devoted to one specific task, such as solving a complex mathematical equation or forecasting weather patterns. A **mainframe**, although it is large like a supercomputer, is usually dedicated to processing hundreds of different tasks simultaneously.

Microcomputers

A **microcomputer** is any computer smaller than a mainframe, ranging from a large Web server all the way down to a handheld organizer.

There are three main types of microcomputers:

■ Desktops

The name says it all. A **desktop computer** is a microcomputer made to sit on or beside a desk. Usually, a desktop computer has the monitor, keyboard, and mouse as separate components. (See Peripherals on page 13.)

■ Laptops (notebooks)

A **laptop computer** is designed to fit comfortably on the user's lap as well as on top of a desk. The keyboard, mouse, and screen are usually built into the unit, with the screen folding down for easy storage. Laptops are also referred to as portable computers and notebooks.

■ Handhelds

A **handheld organizer** is a small computer, less powerful than a desktop or a laptop, designed to be held in one hand while you operate it. Typically, you use a stylus (pen-like tool) to write on the handheld's screen. Handheld computers are also called "organizers" because they originated from digital "assistants," used for keeping track of meetings, phone numbers, addresses, notes, and e-mail. Now handheld computers have become powerful enough to run many different types of programs, from video games to office software. One of the more popular brands of handhelds is the Palm series by Palm, Inc. A handheld is also called a palmtop or personal digital assistant (PDA).

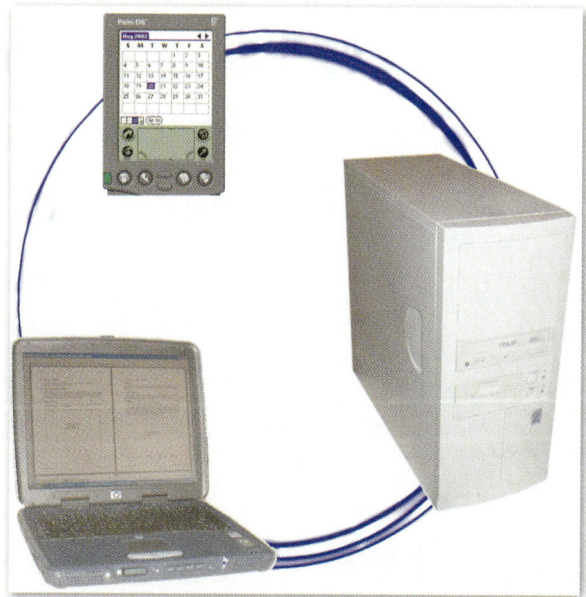

What Is Hardware?

Hardware represents all the physical parts of the computer, including anything inside or outside the computer, from the smallest microchip to the metal case that holds it all together. The term system unit refers to the computer itself and everything inside. Peripherals, which are connected to the outside of the system unit, are separate devices controlled by, or used to control, the computer.

Hardware is the real, physical part of the computer; however, a computer also needs software to control its hardware. Software consists of the programs that run on the computer, including applications, which perform necessary tasks, and the operating system, which allows the programs on a computer to communicate with the hardware.

Microcomputer Hardware Components

The system unit of a computer represents the main part of a computer and includes all the hardware inside the "box." Peripherals make up the rest of the hardware, which connects at specific places on the outside of the system unit. Peripherals are used for transmitting data in and out of the computer.

System Unit

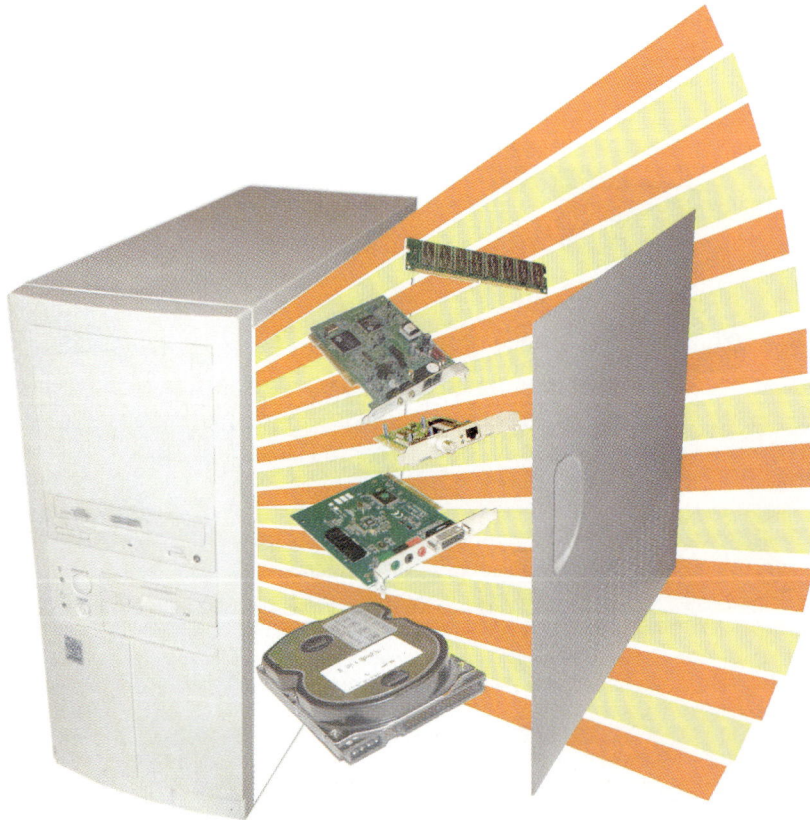

- System case

The system case (known as the "tower" in upright desktop models, or simply the "box") holds everything together. It contains the power supply, and all the brackets and slots to hold the other system unit components (such as a hard drive, or a video card).

- Motherboard

The motherboard is the large circuit board that connects all the individual components inside a system unit, most notably the processor and the RAM.

- Processor

Think of the processor (or *central processing unit* — CPU) as the brain of the computer. Every time a program or piece of hardware calculates something, it uses the processor to do it. You can measure these calculations in millions per second, so the faster the processor, the faster the computer. (However, the other system unit components can affect the overall speed of the computer as well.)

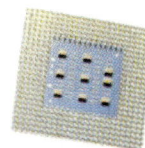

- RAM

If the computer's processor is the brain, the RAM is its short-term memory. RAM is an acronym for random access memory. Each program uses RAM to store temporary data when it runs, allowing it to perform tasks faster. The more RAM a computer has, the more programs it can run at one time and the faster they will perform. This data is only temporary, since any information saved by programs into RAM is lost when the computer is turned off.

- Hard drive

The hard drive is the long-term memory of the computer. Files, programs — anything made up of data — all are stored on the hard drive if they have to be preserved when the computer is turned off. The size of files on a hard drive is usually measured in kilobytes (KB) or megabytes (MB), whereas the size of a hard drive is often measured in gigabytes (GB). One gigabyte equals roughly one thousand megabytes, and a megabyte is around a thousand kilobytes. A kilobyte is around a thousand bytes (a byte being the smallest unit in which data is organized).

Each drive, both hard drives and removable storage drives (see below) are always assigned letters to identify them in the computer. The drive letter assigned to the main hard drive on a computer is almost always **C**.

- Graphics

The graphics card transforms graphical data into images that the user can understand. The monitor connects to the graphics card to receive the images.

- Removable storage

Sometimes you have to take data with you. Removable storage means that your data is stored on an object that can be connected to your computer to receive the data and then connected to another computer so you can read the data at that location. There are many different types of removable storage. Four of the most common types are described here:

- Floppy disk

A floppy disk is the smallest medium for storing data. A typical floppy disk holds 1.44 MB of data. Floppy disks are called "floppy" because the data is stored on a thin (and floppy) magnetic disc inside the hard plastic shell.

- CD-ROM/CD-Writer

A CD-ROM is a compact disk that contains data or programs instead of music. A typical CD-ROM can contain up to 650 MB of data. A computer needs a CD-ROM drive to read CDs. A CD-ROM drive is standard in almost all computers.

CD-R stands for **CD-R**ecordable. This type of compact disc can have data recorded on it (but only once) using a CD-writer drive. Most CD-Rs hold from 650 to 800 MB of data. Writing data to a CD-R is called "burning a disk," because the CD-writer uses a laser to write the data onto the surface of the CD-R.

CD-RW stands for **CD-ReW**ritable. This type of compact disk can have data written to it more than once using a special CD-RW drive. When a CD-RW disk is full, it can be erased and you can start writing data to it again, or you can add to existing data if there is enough space on the CD-RW disk.

- Zip disk

Similar to a floppy disk, a Zip disk is a removable disk that stores data. However, a Zip disk has much more space, with disks available that hold either 100 MB or 250 MB of data. You need a Zip drive to be able to use Zip disks.

- DVD

Not just for playing movies, DVDs can also hold data — the average capacity being around 4.7 GB. Soon all software may be distributed on DVDs instead of CDs because programs are becoming larger. The demand for DVD-Rs (recordable DVDs) is increasing as well.

• Sound

Most computers come equipped with a soundcard, enabling programs to provide audio. Audio sources include music files on the computer, Internet radio, music and sound effects from a video game, or the DVD movie you're watching.

• Modem

A modem (MOdulator DEModulator) is a device that converts data from the digital format to an analog format that can be used to transfer data between two computers via phone lines and cable. You may need a modem to connect a computer to the Internet. The most common speed for a modem is 57,600 bps, or 56K.

- Network interface

In these days of high-speed Internet access, sometimes a modem isn't enough to get your computer online. High-speed Internet access, like cable or DSL, requires a network card to connect to your computer. A network card allows a computer to connect with a network, and it is what the computer uses to transmit and receive data to and from the network.

Peripherals

Peripherals are hardware devices that attach to the outside of the computer. Usually, a peripheral is an input-output device — that is, a device used to put data into the computer (such as a keyboard for entering data), or output data to a form you can use (such as a printer, which takes data documents and prints them in a readable form).

- Keyboard

The keyboard is an essential data input device and has been around since the early days of the computer. When you type words or numbers using the keyboard, the computer stores them as data.

- Mouse

A mouse is a graphical way of communicating with your computer. It is named after the rodent because it is small and round and is connected to the computer by a wire resembling a tail. Every computer has a little arrow onscreen called the pointer. When the mouse moves, the pointer moves. A mouse can have from one to three buttons, so that the pointer can be moved around to interact with objects on the screen.

- Scanner

A scanner is used to copy images directly into your computer. A drawing or a photograph is placed on the glass plate of the scanner, which then makes a copy of the image and saves it as a graphics file on your computer.

- Other input devices

The mouse and the keyboard are the most tried-and-true of the input devices, but there are many other specialized devices that work well for specific situations. The light pen can be used to draw directly onto the screen of a computer. The tablet is used much the same way: You draw on a sensor tablet with a special stylus. The touch-screen, a staple of kiosks and bank machines, enables you to use your finger on the screen to input commands to the computer. The barcode scanner, a distant relative of the photo scanner (described on p. 13), reads the barcodes printed on paper or consumer products. This is often used for taking inventory, when connected to a portable computer (a laptop or a PDA).

- Monitor

The monitor is an output device that allows the computer to display visual information to the user. It displays words, numbers, and pictures on its screen to help you navigate in the programs and interact with the computer.

- Printer

As mentioned previously, a printer prints documents that are on your computer onto paper. The two most common types of printers available today are inkjet and laser printers. An inkjet printer prints color or black-and-white, and uses ink to print on the paper. A laser printer most commonly prints in black-and-white, although color laser printers are available. Laser printers use toner to print, like a photocopier, and print faster than inkjet printers, but are also generally more expensive.

- Speakers

If a computer has a soundcard (and most do), you'll need speakers to actually hear the sound. Some computers come with speakers built in, usually as part of the monitor or system unit. If not, you can use external computer speakers, which are smaller than most hi-fi systems and often not as powerful. But they do work well for most audio coming from your computer, and because audio is such a big part of computer applications (especially video games and music software), speakers are becoming an essential peripheral.

Universal Serial Bus

Arguably one of the most important advances in PC computer technology since the Pentium processor, **Universal Serial Bus** (USB) is changing the way external peripherals connect to the computer. USB represents a simple way of connecting any computer peripheral (mouse, keyboard, printer, scanner, digital camera, soundcard, and so on.) to the computer, using only a single cable. In addition to being simple to connect, USB devices are hot-swappable (which means they can be plugged in or unplugged while the computer is turned on), and can draw a small amount of electricity from the computer, which means certain peripherals don't even need to plug in to an AC/DC outlet to work.

Prior to the introduction of USB in 1996, connecting a new piece of external hardware for the first time was a difficult task. You had to wrestle with issues like installing an internal adaptor (for instance, a SCSI adaptor), and then you had to sort out details related to port number, IRQ settings, and possibly even DIP switches on the adaptor card.

USB devices are fully "Plug and Play," meaning that you just need to plug the peripheral into a USB port to start using it immediately. For most common peripherals (mouse, keyboard, scanner, and printer), the drivers are already included in the operating system (see Chapter 3 for more details on operating systems), so you might not even need to install additional software. USB's biggest advantage, though, is its scalability. A computer can run up to 127 USB devices simultaneously, although another external peripheral called a USB hub will be needed to accommodate that many connections; most computers come with only two USB ports installed.

COMPUTE THIS: Internal or External Hardware?

When you refer to computer hardware, internal hardware is something that is installed inside the system unit, and external hardware is something that connects to the outside of the computer. Some hardware can only be internal, like RAM or a CPU. Other hardware can only be external, like peripheral devices such as a printer or a scanner. However, a lot of hardware exists in both internal and external form. Each situation offers certain advantages and disadvantages.

Internal hardware:

❖   Can communicate faster with some computer components (especially the CPU.)

❖   Is cheaper (less manufacturing is needed to add things like the casing, and so on.)

❖   Can draw power directly from the system unit's power supply.

External hardware:

❖   Can be more accessible than internal components (no reaching around the back of the computer to change cables). Peripheral devices often include easy-to-read lights and displays that can help you know exactly what the hardware is doing (especially useful if something goes wrong).

❖   Can be more rugged than internal components (that outside casing isn't just for decoration).

❖   Can draw power from an external power source (such as an AC adaptor), reducing the strain on the computer's internal power supply and keeping the temperature down inside the system unit. Internal hardware throws off a small amount of heat, which in turn can affect the CPU's performance.

❖   Is usually more expensive than internal hardware of the same quality.

❖   Is often easier to install if it connects to the computer with a USB cable.

When it comes to buying hardware, think carefully about how you are going to use it. For example, if you're going to leave the modem plugged into the phone line all the time and will be using the Internet connection only for casual net surfing, an internal modem is good enough. If you might be moving the modem between different computers, or connecting it to different phone lines, an external modem would be more useful. External modems also have lights on the front indicating what the modem is doing at any given second. If you need to use the Internet connection for business purposes, those lights are indispensable in troubleshooting connection problems and thus helping you get back online as soon as possible.

Operating Systems

- **Overview**
- **Types of Operating Systems**
- **Operating System Tasks**

OBJECTIVES: When you have finished this chapter, you will be able to define what an operating system is. You will also be familiar with some of the main tasks performed with operating system software.

Overview

When you are using a computer, you are actually using at least two programs at one time: the **operating system** (OS) and a software **application**, such as a word processor or a DVD player. The operating system is the most important program on the computer. It communicates between the computer hardware, such as the keyboard, the mouse, or the processor and the application you are using, such as the word processor. Without an operating system, the computer and the application are useless.

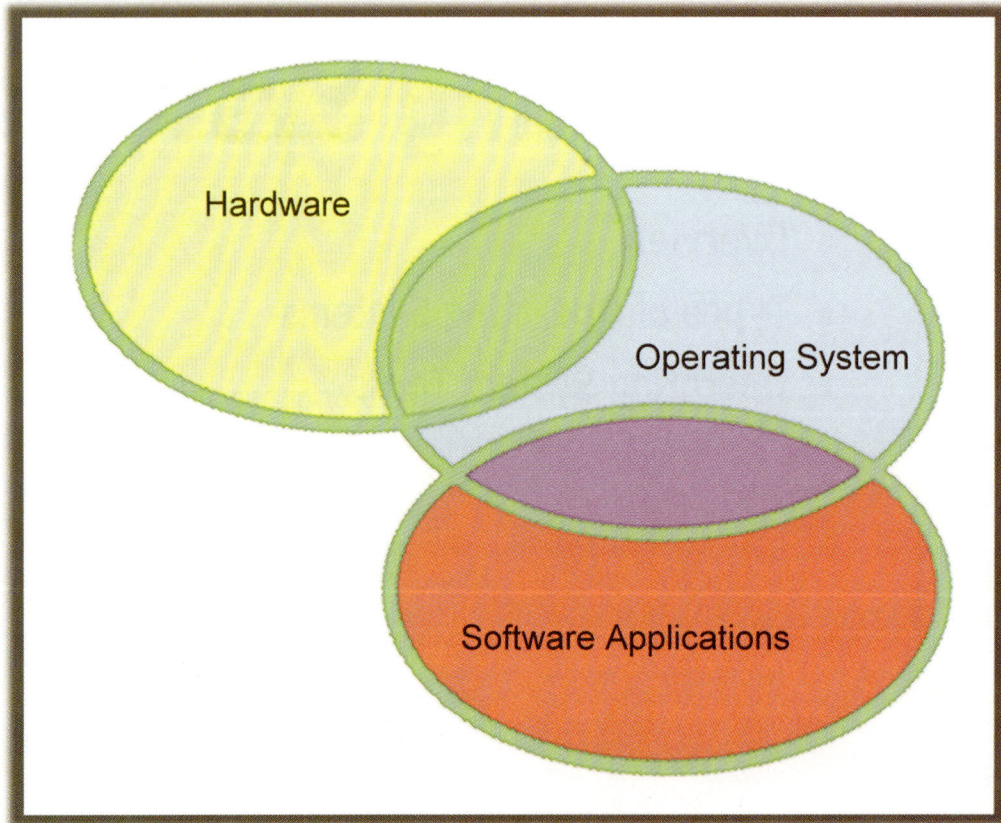

Hardware

Operating System

Software Applications

Types of Operating Systems

There are many operating systems available for computers. Which operating system you use will determine how you work with the computer, how programs look, and especially which applications you use. Most software developers produce software for only one operating systems, so the choice of the operating system is important. The three operating systems listed in the following sections are the most common.

Windows

Without quoting numbers, it's safe to say that Windows is the most common operating system available. At the time this book was written, Windows was at version 5.1, more commonly known as Windows XP. With its built-in networking capabilities, Windows seems to remain popular.

A Windows computer is referred to as a PC-compatible, or a PC. Windows works only with PC-compatible hardware.

A typical Windows XP screen might look like this:

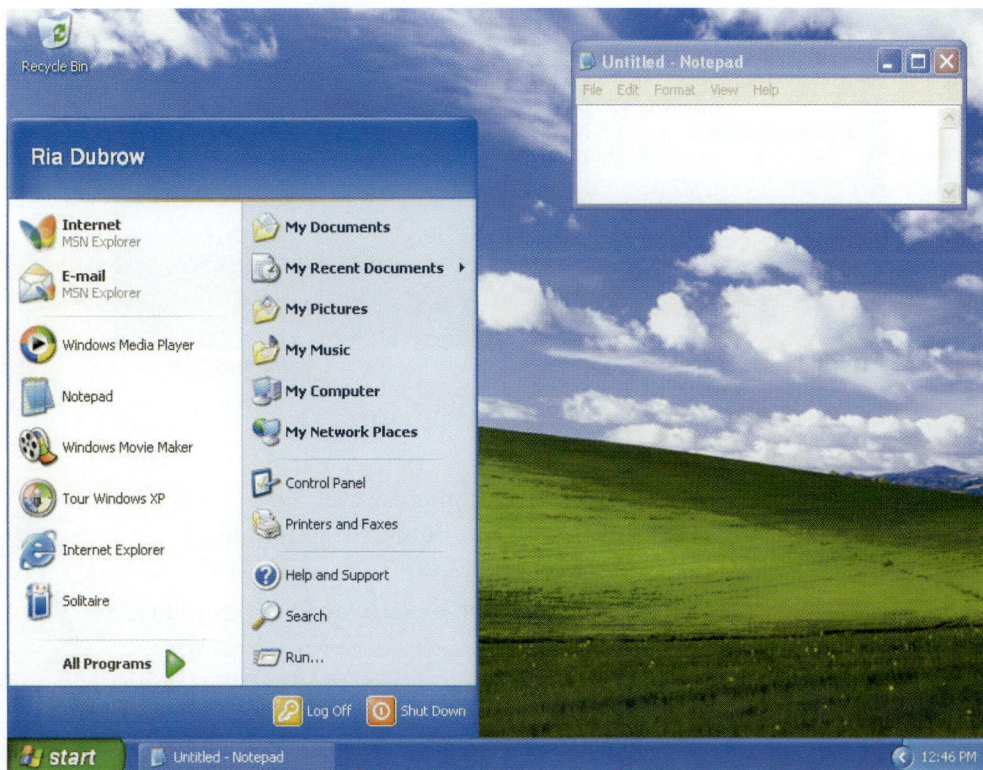

There have been many versions of Windows. Windows 3.1, Windows 95, Windows 98, and Windows ME were designed mainly for home users. Windows NT, and Windows 2000 were meant more for office networks. They handled programs differently than the other versions. Both types of the operating system have been combined into one in Windows XP, which has two versions: Windows XP Home Edition, for private users, and Windows XP Professional, for business users and offices.

Macintosh

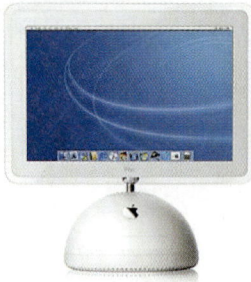

The Macintosh operating system, manufactured by Apple Computers, Inc., is another OS with a long history. The Macintosh OS runs only on Macintosh-compatible hardware, such as the iMac (shown opposite).

The Macintosh OS is currently at version 10 (Mac OS X). The Macintosh operating system seems to be favored for graphic and multimedia applications.

A typical Macintosh OS X screen might look like this:

Mac OS X Images © Apple

Linux

The Linux operating system is available in commercial and "open source" versions. Open source means that the OS is a public programming project. Programmers can download the files used to create the OS (the "source files") from the Internet and improve them in any way they like, provided that they make the improved version available for others to download. In general, Linux is not an operating system for beginners and is fairly complex to set up. However, this complexity comes with an advantage: exact control over how the operating system works and what it does.

Because of the small number of commercial developers, the Linux operating system has fewer applications available than Windows or Macintosh. However, it is growing in popularity, so this could change with time.

PDA Operating Systems

Desktop and laptop computers aren't the only microcomputers that require an operating system. The handheld computers (PDAs or "palmtops") also run programs and require an operating system with which to run them. The two most common palmtop operating systems (at time of writing) are the PalmOS (by Palm, Inc.) and Windows CE (used in the Pocket PC).

A typical Palm OS 3.5 screen might look like this:

What's Next?

Never content with keeping the status quo, the software companies creating operating systems continue to rewrite and revise their software constantly. One such initiative, which you may have already heard of, is Microsoft .NET.

At its core, .NET is an improved platform for developing software. Among other innovations, .NET is geared towards creating and running Web services. Web services are programs, which, thanks to the implementation of certain open data standards (such as XML), can easily exchange data with other programs, regardless of operating system. What this means is that in the future as more and more operating systems, programs, and Web services are created with .NET, networking and communicating between programs running different operating systems will become even easier than it is today. Who knows? Perhaps soon even the divisions between individual operating systems will start to blur.

Operating System Tasks

A computer's operating system is more than a transparent platform for running programs. You can also use it for performing many different computer tasks, ranging from turning the computer on or off and organizing files, to hardware maintenance and diagnostics. A few of these tasks will be examined more closely in the following pages.

Note: From this point on, this book is intended for users of Windows, and all examples will be demonstrated using the Windows XP Professional operating system.

File Management

Data stored on a computer needs to be organized so that you can find the data the next time you need it. Therefore data is stored in **files**. File management on a computer is based on the same principles as paper file management in the physical world: data (words, numbers, images, and so on.) is written to a file. This can be a paper document, such as a letter, but it could also be a business presentation, or perhaps a large inventory database. Any number of files can be kept together in a **folder**. A computer hard drive (or a disk, or a CD-R) can hold as many folders and files as space allows.

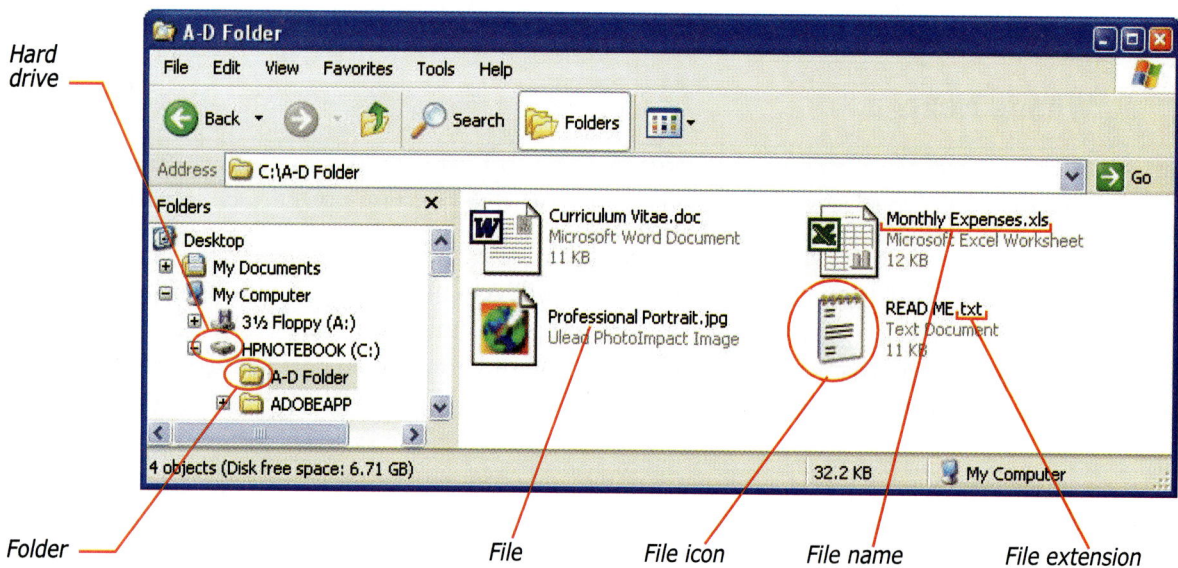

In Windows, the type of a file is usually represented by its icon and its extension, which refers to the last three letters of its filename, prefixed with a period. An "icon" is a small image that the operating system uses to represent files of the same type. For example, all text files are represented by an icon like this: 📄, even though each has different content and a different name.

The icon that Windows assigns to the file matches that file's extension. In the case of the text file in the image on the previous page, the filename is **Readme.txt**, the extension is **.txt**. Almost all files have an extension, even though by default Windows does not display the filename extension.

After files are saved on your computer, and are organized into folders, you can locate them easily. They can be modified, copied, moved, or renamed (to name a few options) in any way you like.

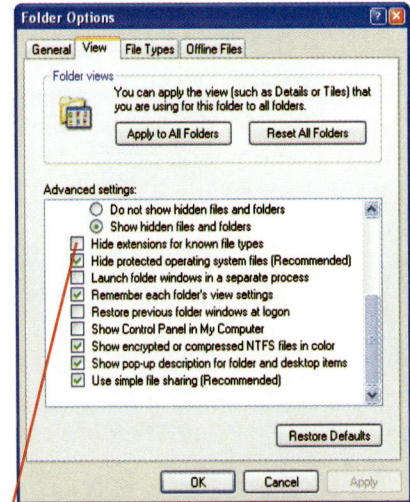

Open a file window on your computer and select Tools > Options to make sure that this option is unchecked if you want to be able to see file extensions.

COMPUTE THIS: Using the Clipboard To Manage Files

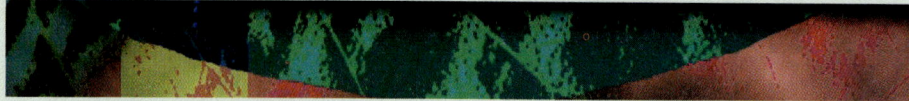

One feature common to almost all operating systems with a graphical user interface is the **Clipboard**. The Clipboard is a place to store data temporarily when you need to make a copy of something or if you need to move part of one file to another. This data can be anything (including elements from inside a file like text, images, and so on.), but often you will find it extremely useful for reorganizing and moving files.

Copy: When you *copy* a file, the original stays where it is on the computer and a copy of it is saved to the Clipboard. It will stay in the Clipboard until another item is copied, or the computer is turned off.

Cut: When you *cut* a file, the original is deleted from the current document, but a copy of it is saved to the Clipboard.

Paste: When you *paste* a file, a copy is placed into the folder currently open; however, this does not empty the Clipboard. In fact, the same item can be pasted as many times as you like, until it has been replaced in the Clipboard by a newer item.

Of course, you are not limited to saving only one file. You can save as many files as you choose to the Clipboard, but they're all copied as a group, if one is pasted, all are pasted. This is what makes the Clipboard so useful for reorganizing files. In three steps, you can move as many files as you want from one folder to another: Select the files, cut them, and then paste them from the Clipboard into the new folder.

System Maintenance

Like cars, computers won't operate perfectly forever; however, there is a certain amount of preventive maintenance you can easily carry out yourself.

■ Defragment

A hard drive in a computer is really a big circle, divided into many tiny sections (called clusters). Files occupy clusters on the disk, and everything works best when all the clusters that make up a particular file sit right next to each other. However, every time the operating system writes a file to the disk, it chooses the next available empty location in the circle. If that location isn't made up of enough clusters to hold the entire file, the disk fills it up and skips ahead to the next empty spot on the disk. When the pieces of a single file are split up among many locations like this, the file is **fragmented**.

A fragmented file takes longer to open or edit, because the hard drive data head has to move all over the place to find each cluster. On one file this isn't a problem, but on dozens or even hundreds of files, this can slow down a computer. The slower speed can cause performance problems, especially when using software that is made up of fragmented files.

To correct this situation, Windows comes with a program called the disk **Defragmenter** that searches for fragmented files and then reorganizes the hard disk so that all parts of a file sit together.

■ Check Disk

Shutting down your computer when Windows is running can cause files to become corrupted. File corruption can also occur if a program crashes. Sometimes, corrupted files also affect the operating system (or in rare cases, the hard drive itself). To keep this from happening (or to fix some types of corrupted files), you should periodically check your hard disk for errors.

COMPUTE THIS: Defrag Your Hard Drive!

It is recommended that you defragment your hard drive at least once every month or so, and even more often if you use the computer to edit large files, such as graphics or audio files.

Depending on the size of your hard drive, a defragmentation can take anywhere from an hour to several hours. Always wait to defragment your hard drive at a time when no one will be using the computer.

1. Double-click the My Computer icon on your Desktop, right-click your hard drive, and select Properties.

2. Click the Tools tab, and then click the Defragment Now button.

3. In the Disk Defragmenter window, you can click the Analyze button to get the Defragmenter to analyze your disk to see if you need to defragment it.

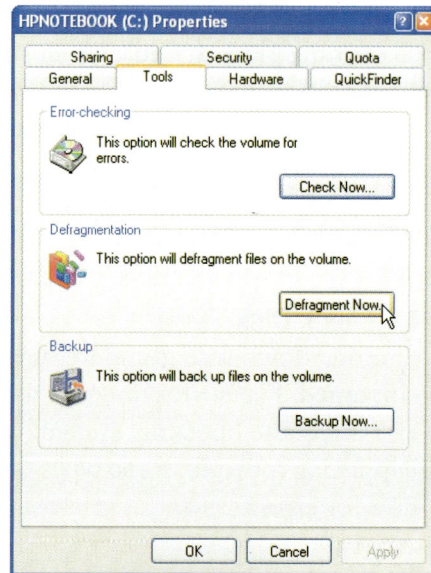

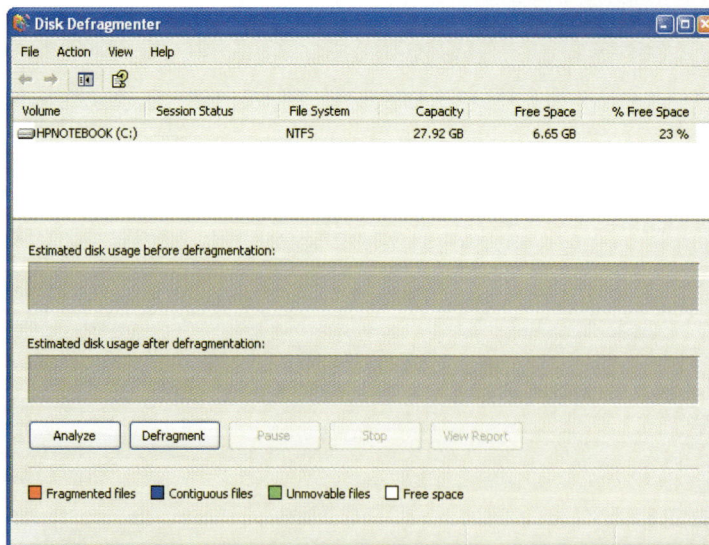

4. Click the Defragment button when you are ready to defragment your hard drive.

COMPUTE THIS: Check Your Disk!

1. Open My Computer, right-click your hard drive, and select Properties.
2. Click the Tools tab, and click the Check Now button.
3. In the Check Disk dialog box, check *Automatically fix file system errors* if you want the program to fix any errors it can, and check *Scan for and attempt recovery of bad sectors* if you want to perform a far more in-depth (but far slower) scan of the actual hard disk.

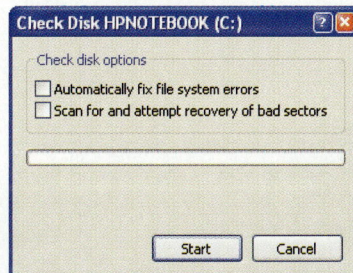

HPNOTEBOOK (C:) Properties

| Sharing | Security | Quota |
| General | Tools | Hardware | QuickFinder |

Error-checking
This option will check the volume for errors.
[Check Now...]

Defragmentation
This option will defragment files on the volume.
[Defragment Now...]

Backup
This option will back up files on the volume.
[Backup Now...]

[OK] [Cancel] [Apply]

Check Disk HPNOTEBOOK (C:)

Check disk options
☐ Automatically fix file system errors
☐ Scan for and attempt recovery of bad sectors

[Start] [Cancel]

4. Click Start to begin checking for errors.

System Monitoring

Not everything that your operating system is currently doing is immediately apparent when you look at the screen. Fortunately, in most operating systems there are ways to monitor this activity. Information you might want to monitor can include programs running, CPU activity, RAM in use, and traffic on a modem or network connection.

COMPUTE THIS: Examining System Resources with the Windows Task Manager

Most operating systems offer you advanced control over how they run. Windows XP provides you with the Task Manager, which can be used for anything from navigating between open applications, to reporting system performance statistics and troubleshooting crashed programs.

Displaying the Task Manager

1. Right-click an empty space on the Taskbar.
2. Select Task Manager.
The Task Manager window opens.

Click the Applications tab to list the applications currently running. You need to use this list when you have to close any applications that might have crashed.

Click the Processes tab to view every single part of all programs that are running on your computer. Use this for advanced troubleshooting.

Click the Performance tab to view a real-time read-out of your computer's processor usage, memory, and other statistics. This window, combined with the Processes window, is useful for troubleshooting programs that might be slowing down your computer.

The Networking tab monitors the data traffic through your network connection, measuring the percentage of the connection's capacity being used.

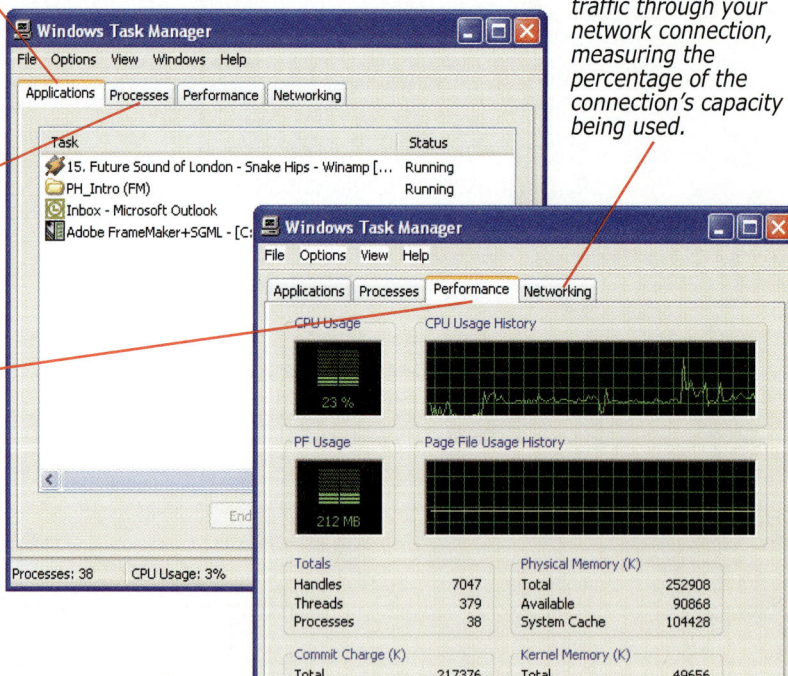

3. Click the close button [X] to close the Task Manager when finished.

Desktop Applications

- **Overview of Application Software**
- **Word Processing**
- **Spreadsheet**
- **Presentation**
- **Database**
- **Contact Management**
- **Utility Software**

OBJECTIVES: When you have finished this chapter, you will be familiar with the many types of computer application software, and their uses. If you have access to a computer, you will also be able to download and install free anti-virus software.

Overview of Application Software

Applications (or programs) are the software "tools" you use on the computer to accomplish a certain task. Usually, applications that might be used together are installed together. This is called a software suite. Smaller applications that carry out a specific task, usually related to the computer or operating system directly, are often called utilities.

The "big five" types of office software are word processing, spreadsheet, presentation, database, and contact management. These are the applications you are most likely to use. However, applications exist for just about any other purpose, professional (project management software, computer assisted drawing — CAD — software for drafting or architecture, 3-D animation rendering software for film, and so on.) or entertainment (video games, music file players, DVD playing software, and so on.), and much, much more.

Word Processing

A **word processor** is an application used to write and edit content that you would read. You can change the look of the text, add pictures, or lay out the page any way you want.

You can use a word processor to write a short story, a business letter, or your autobiography.

Some examples of word processors are Microsoft Word, Corel WordPerfect, and Lotus WordPro.

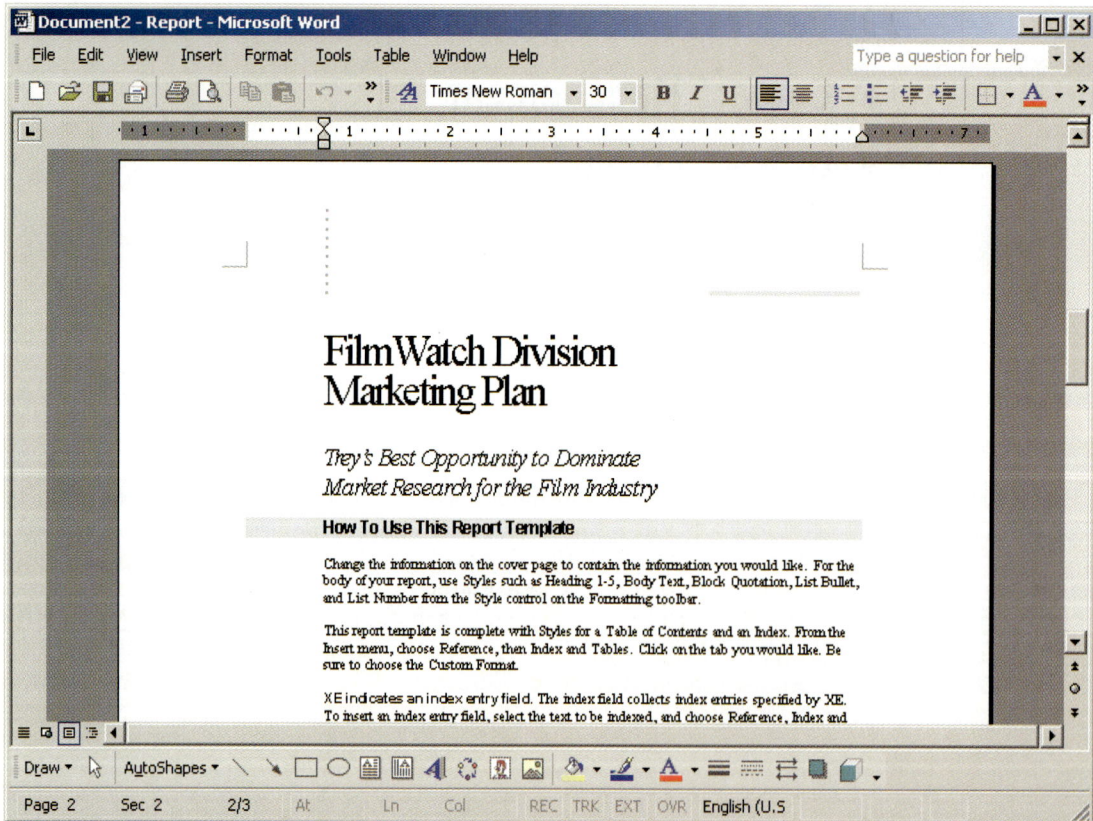

Microsoft Word 2002

COMPUTE THIS: Microsoft WordPad

Even if you don't have the latest version of Microsoft Office or Corel Wordperfect Office, you can still do word processing with this basic word processor that is included in all versions of Windows. Follow these steps to access and use Microsoft WordPad:

Using Microsoft WordPad

1. Click the Start button, and select Start > All Programs > Accessories > WordPad.

2. WordPad enables you to perform many of the page layout and text editing tasks you need to create good-looking documents. The example below indicates some of these tasks.

Cut, copy, paste text

Insert current date/time

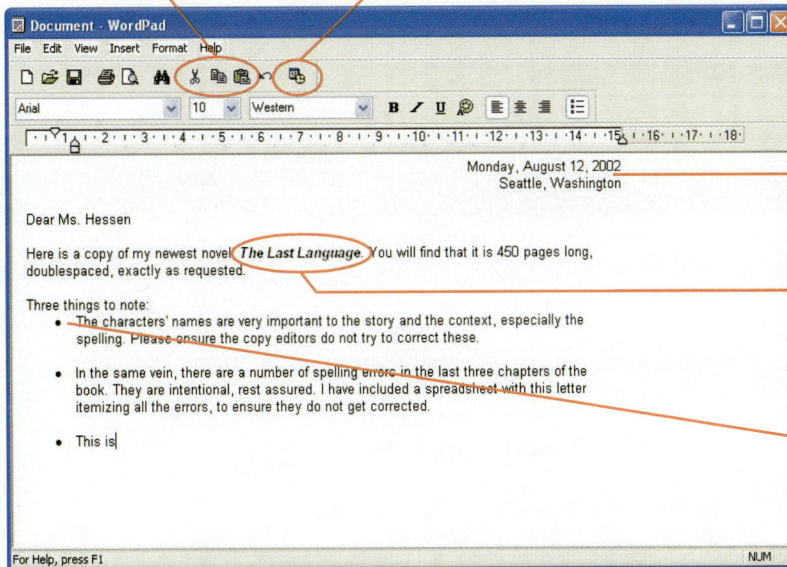

Paint
Program Compatibility Wizard
Synchronize
Tour Windows XP
Windows Explorer
Windows Movie Maker
WordPad

Align text

Format characters (bold, italics, underlining, color)

Bulleted lists

Monday, August 12, 2002
Seattle, Washington

Dear Ms. Hessen

Here is a copy of my newest novel *The Last Language.* You will find that it is 450 pages long, doublespaced, exactly as requested.

Three things to note:
- The characters' names are very important to the story and the context, especially the spelling. Please ensure the copy editors do not try to correct these.

- In the same vein, there are a number of spelling errors in the last three chapters of the book. They are intentional, rest assured. I have included a spreadsheet with this letter itemizing all the errors, to ensure they do not get corrected.

- This is

For Help, press F1

3. WordPad saves these documents as Rich Text Format files (RTF), which means that they can be read and edited by any word processor application if you need to take them elsewhere or if you get another application at a later date.

Spreadsheet

A **spreadsheet** is a large worksheet usually used for working with numbers. You can lay out the sheet any way you want and include any number of complex calculations. Calculations and numbers can also be displayed using many different types of charts.

You can use a spreadsheet to create financial reports, for business accounting, or to track the seasonal hockey pool.

Some examples of spreadsheet software are Microsoft Excel, Lotus 1-2-3, and Corel Quattro Pro.

Microsoft Excel 2002

Presentation

Presentation software is used for creating a multimedia slideshow, usually designed to accompany a live presentation. Slides can contain text, images, animation, and even sound or movies.

You can give a printed version of a slideshow to the audience as a handout, or project the slideshow onto a screen to accompany your presentation.

Some examples of presentation software are Microsoft PowerPoint, Lotus Freelance, and Corel Presentations.

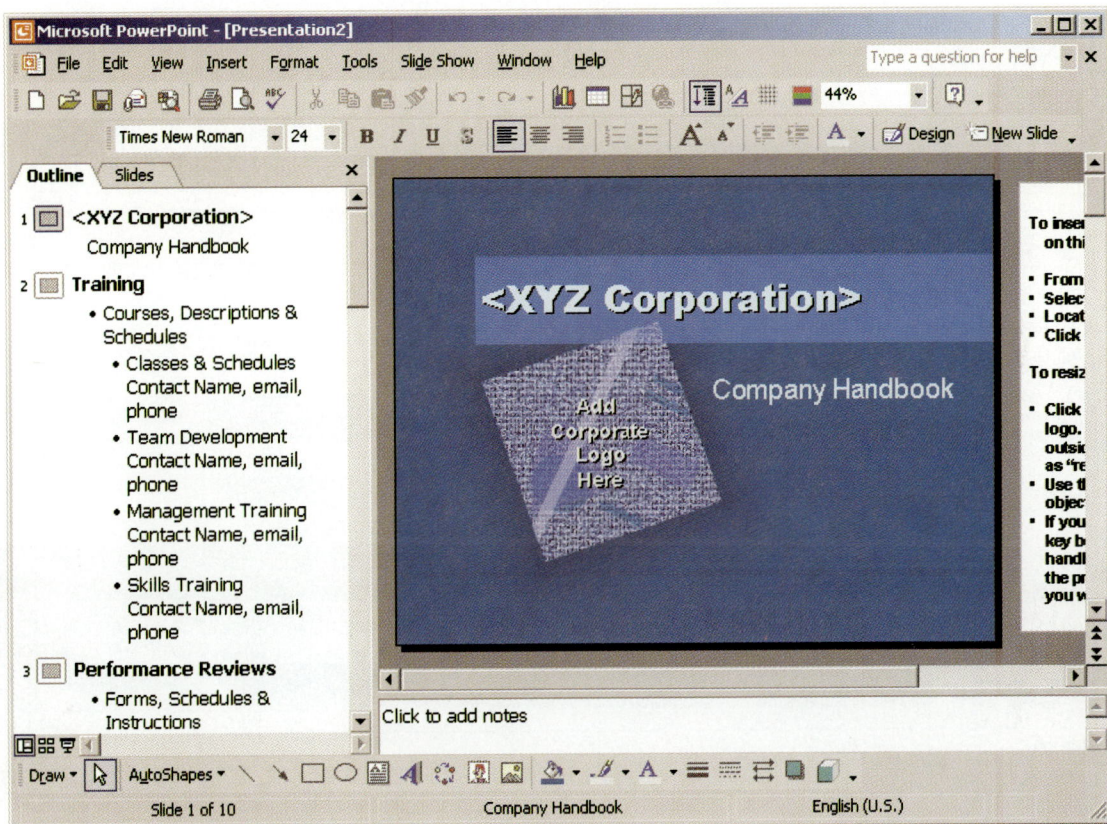

Microsoft PowerPoint 2002

Database

A **database** is used for tracking, storing, sorting, and reporting on data of any kind.

You can use a database for tracking and reporting online sales figures, or keeping track of and searching through a business inventory.

Some examples of database software are Microsoft Access, Lotus Approach, and Corel Paradox.

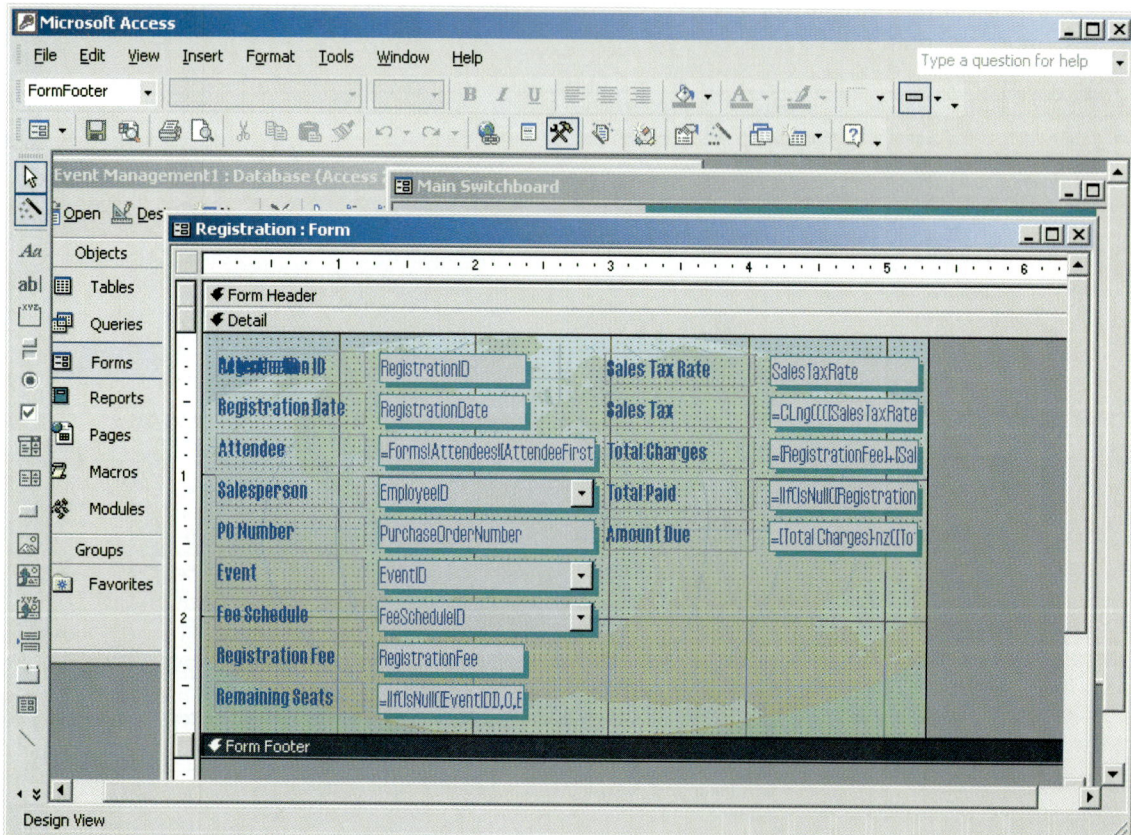

Microsoft Access 2002

Contact Management

Contact management software is used for managing your contact information and it has several elements in common: agenda/calendar, address book, and e-mail. It is also often referred to as a **personal information manager** (PIM).

You can use it to manage names, addresses, and telephone numbers; to keep track of events, such as meetings and appointments; and to send and receive e-mail.

Some examples of contact management software are Microsoft Outlook and Lotus Notes.

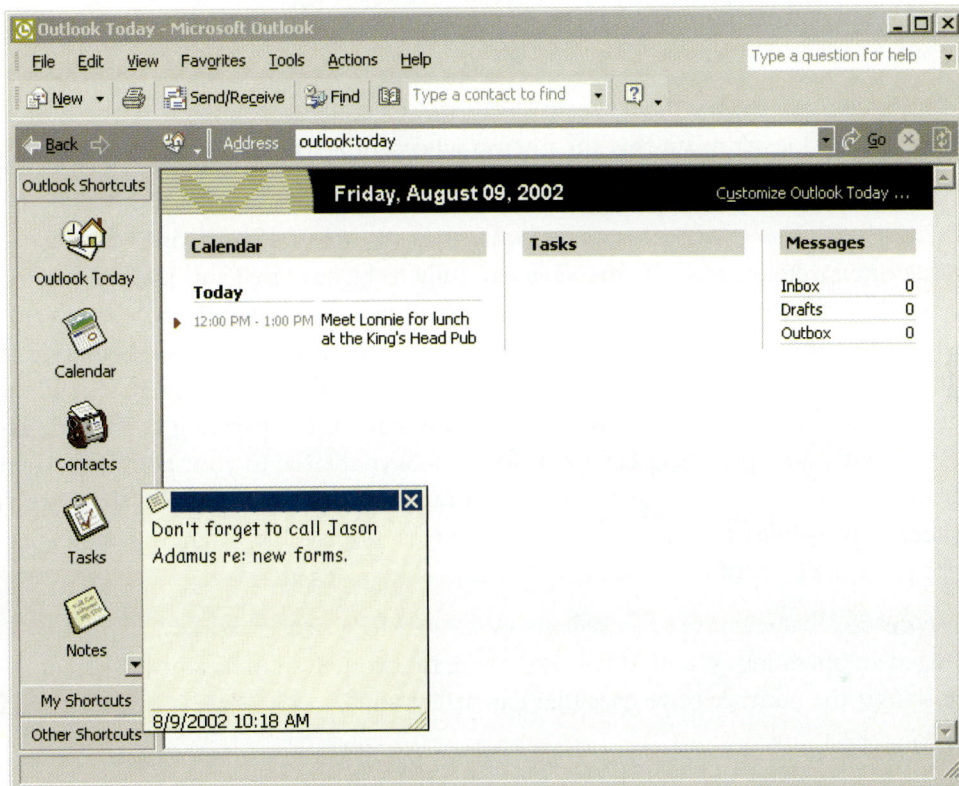

Microsoft Outlook 2002

Utility Software

Software that serves a utilitarian purpose (as opposed to business, entertainment, or creative purposes), is often called a **utility**. Three of the utility applications that are most commonly needed on microcomputers are **anti-virus**, data **backup**, and **file compression**. What they mean and how they work are outlined next.

Anti-Virus Software

■ How do I catch a computer virus?

A computer virus is a program, but instead of being designed to do something useful, it is designed to do annoying (or malicious) things on the user's computer. The damage can range from sending e-mail messages to every person in your address book all the way to crippling your operating system or even deleting everything on your hard drive.

One of the most common way of "catching" a computer virus is by opening a virus-infected file attached to an e-mail message. However, there are more ways than just this for a virus to be unleashed on your computer. Here are a few simple rules you can follow to help keep your computer safe from viruses:

- *Don't open e-mail messages from unknown addresses.* Even if your name is in the header of the e-mail, that doesn't mean that the person who sent it really knows you. If you weren't expecting that e-mail message, don't open it — delete it.

- *Never open a file attached to an e-mail unless you were expecting it.* If someone you trust sends you a file unexpectedly, read the message carefully to be sure that this person was indeed the one who wrote it. Many viruses spread by sending a copy of themselves to every name in the address book of the computer they infect. They usually disguise themselves to look like a regular file of some sort. If you didn't expect the file, don't open it. E-mail the person and ask about it. Wait until they reply that it is safe before opening it. Also, don't let your e-mail software open the attachment for you. Save the file to your hard disk, then open it from a folder there. If the software that should open the file tells you that it can't, then there's a possibility that the file is actually a virus. If it is a file you have been expecting, ask the person who sent it to resend.

- *Always keep your operating system software up to date.* Most viruses work by exploiting a security bug in an operating system. If you make sure that your system has the latest patch installed, you limit the number of viruses that can affect you.

- *Make sure that the security settings in office software and Web browsers are enabled.* Viruses often come in the form of macros, especially in Microsoft Office files. A macro is a small program that runs only inside the program in which it was created. Sometimes macros can execute malicious code, and if one is programmed with a virus, it could harm your system. Make sure that your office software is set to prompt you before running a macro contained by a file. Certain Web sites too can sometimes pass computer viruses on, if the site is programmed by a hacker to attack a Web browser. However, most Web browsers have security preferences to guard against this type of virus, so make sure that these security settings are activated. (See page 60 for more details on Web browser security.)

- *Always format a new floppy disk before using it.* Most manufacturers provide clean disks, but empty floppy disks can contain a virus, though rarely. If you wipe the new floppy clean by formatting it, it will be safe.

■ How does anti-virus software work?

Anti-virus software works by checking all the files on all the drives in your computer to see whether any files match its list of virus descriptions. The descriptions, or virus definitions, are usually maintained and constantly updated by the creator of the anti-virus software. Most anti-virus programs enable you to download new virus definitions online.

Some examples of anti-virus software are Norton Anti-Virus, McAffee VirusScan Online, and Grisoft AVG.

- *Update your virus definitions often!* This is one of the most important rules because new viruses are introduced all the time. The best way to be sure that a sneaky new one doesn't get you is to have your anti-virus software updated. Although once a week is probably a safe bet, you could set the software to check once a day for new virus definitions if you want to be really secure.

COMPUTE THIS: Free Anti-virus Software

Grisoft AVG Anti-virus is anti-virus software that is free to download and use for your personal computer. AVG updates their virus definitions often, so it's economical for keeping your computer virus-free.

Download AVG Anti-Virus

1. Make sure you are connected to the Internet, open Internet Explorer, and go to the following address: **www.grisoft.com**.

2. Click the **Free downloads** link (located on the left-hand side of the page), and then click the **Download AVG Free Edition** link.

3. Scroll down until you see this button [Download AVG Free Edition]; then click it.

4. Click **Yes** to agree to the licence agreement.

5. Fill in the registration form, then click the **Continue** button.
6. You should see a screen that looks like the following. Click the link that will start the download process.

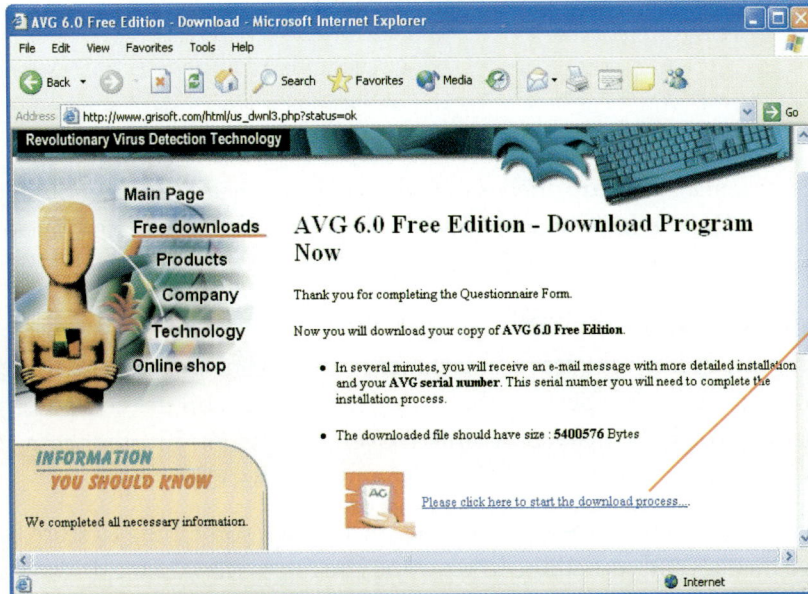

Click here to start downloading the software so that it can be installed on your computer.

7. After the installer file has been downloaded, check your e-mail to open the message sent to you by AVG.
8. Now locate the installer file that you downloaded and double-click it to begin installation. Follow the rest of the instructions outlined in the e-mail to install and configure AVG Anti-virus.

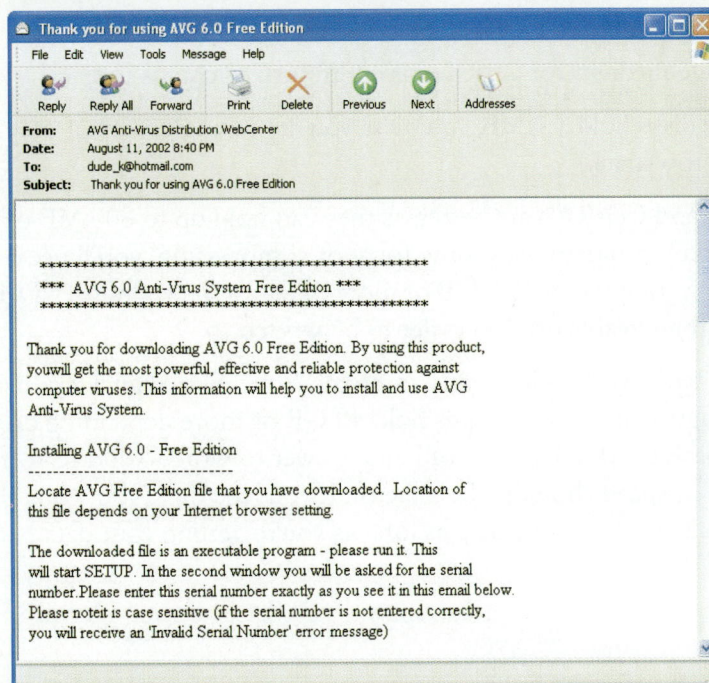

9. Once installed and running, AVG Anti-virus will not only scan your hard drive periodically to search for viruses, it will also connect to the Internet automatically from time to time to update its virus definitions. If you want to change the defaults, the intervals between scans or between updates can be set within the program.

Backup

To back up files, or make a **backup,** means to make a copy of the files or computer programs in case of emergency. In this case, an emergency might result from accidental deletion of files or damage to the hard drive where the files are stored.

■ Why perform a backup?

No computer is perfect, like any piece of machinery or electronics, it can occasionally break down. And no computer user is perfect, the more files you have on the computer, the more likely that something might be deleted or written over by accident. In either case, if the data that was lost is important, you will be glad that you made a backup.

A backup requires three things: software to make the backup, something to store the backup copy on (storage media), and something to write the backup to the storage. If you are backing up a few files, all you need to do is make a copy of them. However, if you want to make regular copies of files from all over your computer or make a copy of your entire computer, then you need specialized backup software to make this copy and then restore it when needed.

Some examples of backup software are Veritas Backup My PC and Roxio GoBack.

■ Storage media

The storage medium for a backup is an important choice too:

- Floppy disks hold 1.4 MB, so unless you are saving copies of only a few individual files, they're too small.

- CD-Rs and CD-RWs are better, as they can hold up to 800 MB of data. However, unless the backup program uses some form of compression, you'll need quite a few CD-Rs to backup a computer with 2 GB or more of data and programs. CD-Rs or CD-RWs require a CD-(re)writeable drive in order to be written to.

- Digital tapes work well for larger systems. You need a digital tape drive to write to and read from digital tapes. Some tapes hold 40 GB or more depending on the type of tape, but tapes have the disadvantage of being slower to write to and read from than CD-Rs. However, speed shouldn't be a factor, if you lose data, you won't care how slow your backup is to restore the data as long as you're getting your data back!

Some recommendations for backup rules: If you do feel you need to back up your computer files, make a backup often! In particular, back up your computer just before you install new software. New software may cause problems with existing software, and the only way to get things working again will be to restore your computer to the way it was before the software was installed.

Also, store your backup media (tapes, CDs, and so on.) in a different place than your computer. If the room that your computer is in is damaged, or if the computer is stolen, there's a fair chance that the backup media will be lost too. Storing your backup copy elsewhere means that even if the whole computer is lost, you can still get a new computer and restore things to the way they were. For people who use their computer for business purposes, this is a cardinal rule.

What is File Compression?

Compression means to make a copy of data, but in a way that takes up less space than usual. For example, an audio file can be saved to a compressed format that takes up only 10 percent of the original size. Some types of files (graphics, audio, and so on.) have their own specialized uncompressed and compressed formats (JPG, MP3, and so on.).

However, there are also generic compression formats than can be used on any file, though the effectiveness of the compression varies from file to file. ZIP is one such compression method, and is the most popular compressed file format for Windows. Compressed file archives, or Zip files, are useful in that they not only shrink files to a much smaller size, but also many individual files can be compressed into one Zip file.

Although Zip files take up far less storage space on the hard drive than their uncompressed counterparts, zipped files cannot be used unless they are "unzipped" (uncompressed) back to their original file type. This means that compression is best used for storing (great for backups) or transporting files when you're not using them, but when the files are needed, they have to be uncompressed again.

Some examples of compression utilities include WinZip, WinRAR, and Stuffit.

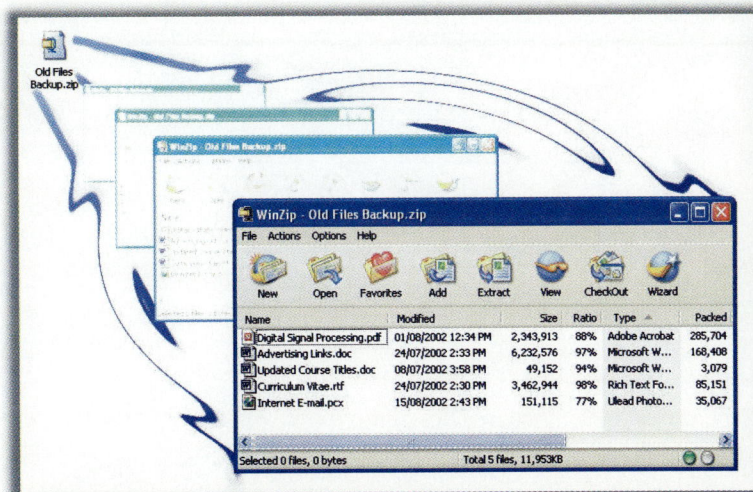

Networks

- **Overview**
- **Types of Networks**
- **Advantages of a Network**

OBJECTIVES: When you have finished this chapter, you will be able to define what a network is and does, and be able to list the advantages to networking computers.

Overview

A **network** is made up of two or more computers connected together, so that users can share data and resources. Computer peripherals, such as printers or external CD-writers, can also be connected to the network, making them available to all users on the network. A computer lab with all the computers connected to the same printer is one example of a network. The Internet (see Internet on page 48) is another type of network, on a much larger scale.

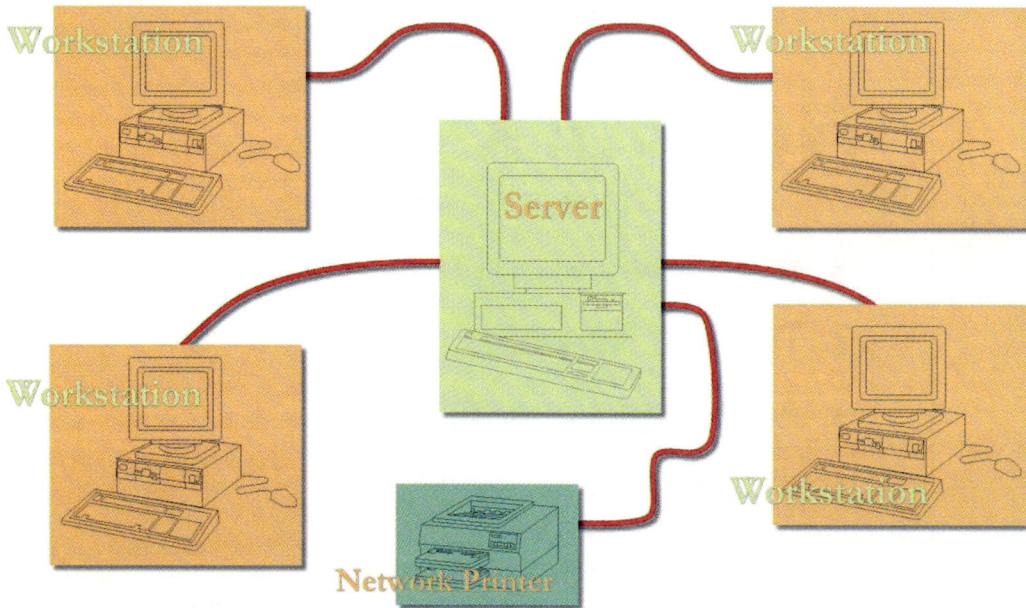

In general, the average network consists of a server, several workstations, and perhaps some peripherals. The server is the main computer on the network, handling network security, storing files (a "file server"), transferring e-mail (an "e-mail server"), or hosting Web pages (a "Web server"). Workstations are the "regular" computers that are connected to the network to take advantage of the benefits it offers. The peripherals can be any devices that can be shared on a network, usually a printer, a scanner, or some type of removable storage.

Types of Networks

Networks are defined mainly by their size and the way in which they are connected, as well as by their topology (the shape of a network, such as bus, ring, or star topology). Although network topology is not covered here, if we examine the ways in which networks can be connected, we can define three main types of networks:

- LAN stands for Local Area Network. A LAN is a network spread out over a short distance, usually inside one room, or one floor of an office. This size limitation is due to the hardware used to connect the parts of the network.

- A Wide Area Network (WAN) is like a LAN, but specialized hardware (like routers, hubs, and so on.) allows the Wan to connect more than one LAN to make one large network. A WAN usually spans a large distance, such as across a college campus or between cities.

- A wireless network is identical to a LAN in many ways, except that the computers are not physically connected to each other. Instead, they communicate via a wireless network card. This type of network is more versatile than a wire-based LAN. For example, a laptop could connect to a wireless network from any position inside an office; however, the wireless range is relatively short — perhaps 100 to 200 feet.

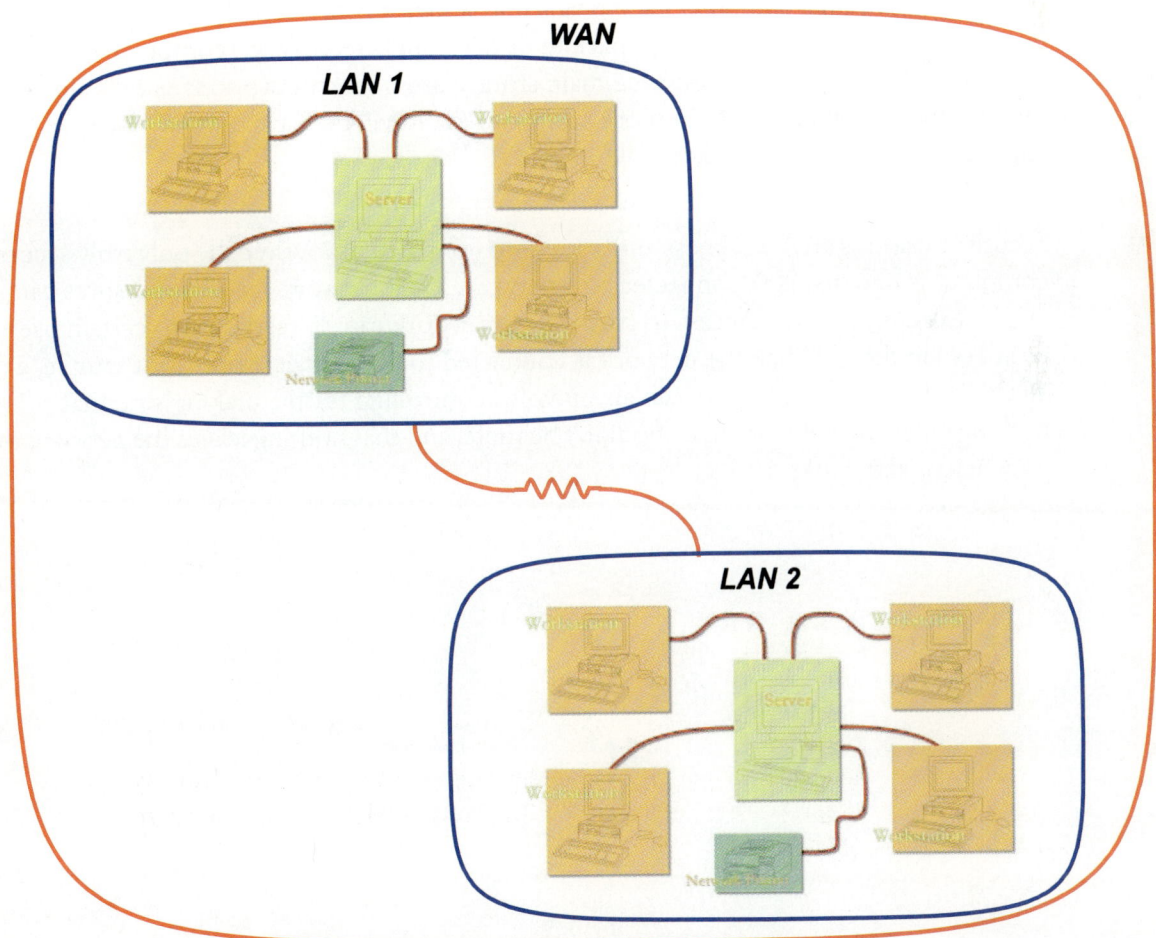

Advantages of a Network

Working on a network of computers provides a number of advantages to the user.

- Access to resources

  Perhaps the most important advantage to connecting computers to form a network is the access to resources. Through a workstation on a network, you have access to peripherals connected to other computers such as a printer, or an external CD-writer (provided they are "shared" on the network, of course). You can also have access to data files stored in a public place on the network, and in many cases you can add your own files to the network storage. This is ideal for sharing information, or collaborating on a project with another person on the network.

  Accessing resources through a network also permits fast access to files, reducing the time spent copying files to and from CD or disk, or physically transporting data and documents from one place to another.

  Most importantly, cost is a big improvement thanks to these shared resources. For example, if every user on a network is sharing the same printer, only the printer needs to be purchased.

- Backup

  Any data stored on a computer can be valuable, and if it is accidentally deleted, that can be very serious. Instead of having a backup device connected to each computer, only one such device is needed to back up the main storage areas on a network. If users store all their important data and files in those storage areas, it will be backed up in case of emergency.

- Security

  Security measures are a weakness and a strength for a network. While the only truly secure computer is one that isn't connected to a network at all, network security measures can still be extremely useful. Access to parts of the network can be restricted to certain users or at certain times. When the network is connected to another network (for example, a WAN or the Internet) security can also involve controlling traffic, making sure that nothing enters the network that shouldn't be there, and that nothing leaves the network to go where it shouldn't.

Internet

- **Overview**
- **Internet Access**
- **World Wide Web**
- **E-mail**
- **Security and Privacy**
- **Search Tools**
- **Common Portals**

OBJECTIVES: When you have finished this chapter, you will be able to define what the Internet is, and how to access it. You will be familiar with various types of Internet software, and their uses. You will also learn the principles of searching for information on the World Wide Web.

Overview

The **Internet** is the largest computer network in the world. Millions of people connect to it every day to find information, exchange e-mail messages, and communicate in many different ways with people all over the world.

This chapter will examine how to get on to the Internet and what you can do there, as well as offer suggestions about what to watch out for.

Internet Access

To connect to the Internet, you need three things: an account with an Internet Service Provider (ISP), the computer hardware that your ISP requires to make the connection (depending on the type of connection your account provides), and Internet software (such as an e-mail reader or a Web browser).

Your ISP is the company you pay for your time connected to the Internet (or time online). Some ISPs charge by the hour (usually for telephone connections), some charge a flat monthly rate (telephone connection, or cable/DSL), and others might even charge rates based on how much data you download from the Internet.

The type of account you choose depends primarily on how much time you think you will spend online. If you will be connecting to the Internet only sporadically to check e-mail or visit an occasional Web site, an hourly-rate dial-up connection may suit you best. If you could be using the Internet often, a flat monthly rate (either for a telephone or a high-speed cable/ DSL connection) would be best. In addition, if you know you will be sending and receiving a lot of data, a (high-speed) cable or DSL connection type will probably be the best choice.

Modem

A modem connection, or "dial-up" account requires a modem connected to your computer. The modem, which is essentially a telephone for the computer, must be connected to a telephone line. Hence the name "dial-up," as the modem quite literally dials the ISP's telephone number to link up to the modem at the other end of the line.

At time of writing, the fastest modem is 57,600 bps (bits-per-second), or "56K." Any new computer that is purchased with a modem will most likely have a 56K modem installed.

Cable/DSL

Cable and DSL connections are known as "high-speed" connections, and for good reason. Cable and DSL speeds are usually around 1.5 Mega-bps (1.5 million bits-per-second) — that's over 26 times as fast as a dial-up Internet connection.

Access Speeds

Having a connection at 56K or 1.5 Mbps, doesn't mean that you will get that speed 100 percent of the time. Those numbers refer to the speed of the connection between your computer and the ISP. However, the true speed of the download depends on the rest of the Internet, how much traffic there is between you and the site, and how busy the site you're visiting is.

If you think your Internet connection is too slow, try visiting a connection speed test site (such as www.testmyspeed.com). When you visit the page, it will run a quick test and tell you the speed at which your connection was operating when the page was loaded.

World Wide Web

When people refer to something being "on the Internet," they usually mean that it is available on the **World Wide Web**. The Web (also called WWW) is a vast network of sites and pages, linked together in different ways, presenting text and images, as well as audio or even video. Web sites can be used for almost anything: marketing for a company, a fan site for a music group, a bulletin board providing information for expectant mothers, or an online bookstore. The following image shows a typical commercial Web site.

The word that is key to understanding how the World Wide Web works is "hyperlink." A hyperlink is a virtual connection to another place on the Web. You click the hyperlink, and the page that is the link's target is displayed. One page is connected to another, which leads to others, which each lead to more, and so on until you have lines intersecting with many other lines. This is similar to the threads of a spider's web; hence the name "World Wide Web."

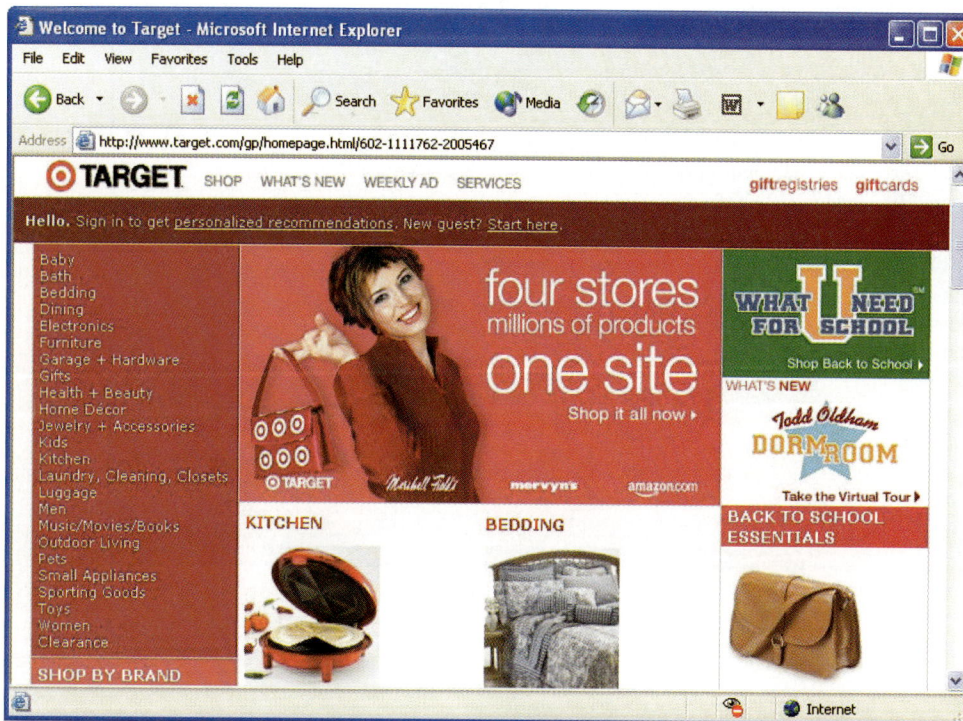

The Target Web site: here you can browse for product information, consult advertisements, and buy products online.

To access the World Wide Web, you need a software program known as a Web browser. This program enables you to browse the content of the WWW and view Web sites. The three most commonly used Web browsers are examined on the next two pages.

URL: Uniform Resource Locator — the technical term for a Web site address. The following URL is divided into three parts: the protocol, the site, and the domain.

http://www.target.com/

The protocol: http stands for Hypertext Transfer Protocol, and is the standard for Web sites.

The site: www is the standard site name for a Web site.

The domain: The first part, target, indicates the domain name. The suffix, .com, is a standard suffix.

Domain Suffixes

You've already seen **.com**, which is still probably the most common (and sought-after) domain name suffix for a Web site. There are also many other standard suffixes: **.edu** (for educational institutions like universities), **.gov** (for U.S. government sites), **.org** (for organizations), **.mil** (for U.S. military sites), **.net** (for networks), and **.biz** (for business sites), to name a few. Most countries also have their own Internet domain suffix: **.ca** (Canada), **.uk** (United Kingdom), **.au** (Australia), **.fr** (France), **.jp** (Japan), etc.

Internet Explorer

If you have Windows installed, you have **Internet Explorer** because it is built into Windows. Open any window, type in an Internet Web address, and Internet Explorer is right there. The previous image is an example of what a typical Internet Explorer screen looks like.

Netscape

The next most popular Web browser, and one of the oldest Web browsers online is **Netscape**. It can be downloaded free from www.netscape.com. Netscape 7, the most current version (at press time), is not just a Web browser. It is really an all-round communications package for the Internet, which includes e-mail as well as chat software and Internet radio (among other features).

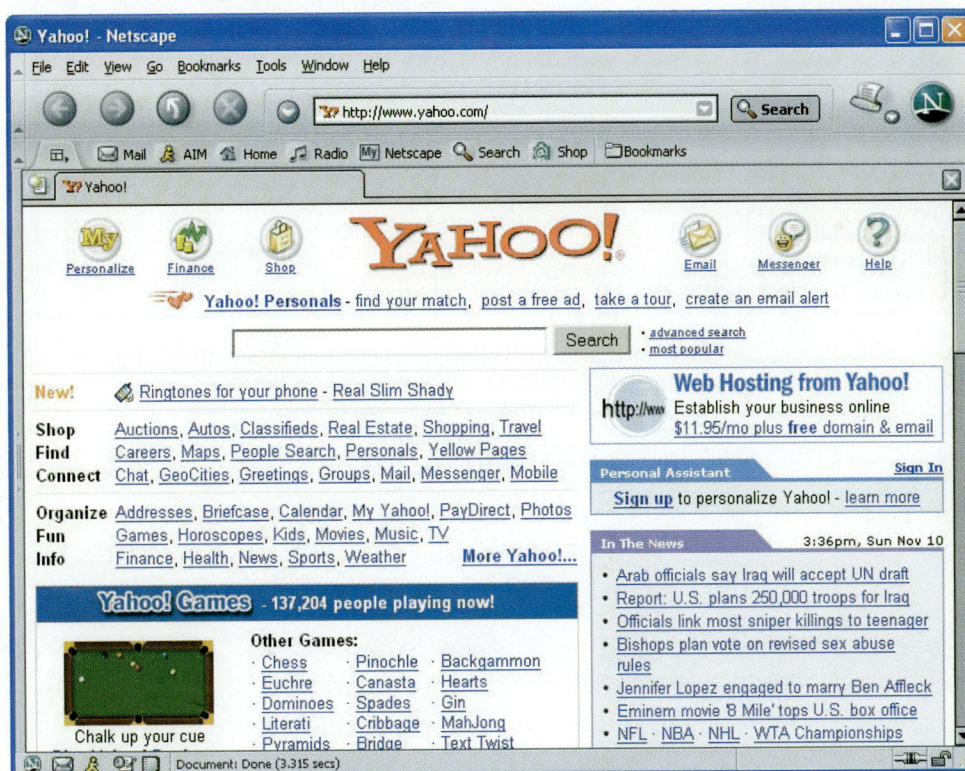

Opera

Another Web browser seems to be gaining in popularity is **Opera**. It claims to be a faster, more flexible browser with strong security, and it offers versions for more than seven different operating systems.

At time of writing, a free version of Opera (with banner advertisements on the toolbar) is available at www.opera.com. Purchasing the full version of Opera removes the banners, giving you more screen area for viewing Web pages.

E-mail

E-mail is a popular use for the Internet. Letters can be sent to anyone else in the world with an e-mail address, and are received almost instantly.

What Can You Do With E-mail?

Other than the obvious advantage of being able to communicate with someone thousands of miles away with little delay, e-mail has other abilities. The best is the ability to add an **attachment** (data files) to an e-mail message. Send digital photographs to your sister across the country, work on the business report while at home and e-mail it back to the head office, or submit that term paper to your professor — these are a few examples of scenarios where you might need to send attachments via e-mail.

Note: Try to avoid sending files that are 2 MB or larger via e-mail. Some mail severs don't allow large e-mails, so if you want to be sure the person on the other end will receive the e-mail, keep it small. Using file compression (see page 41) is a good way to reduce the size of attachment files you send. Also, if you haven't already read it, consult the section on viruses on page 36, e-mail is one of the most common ways for computer viruses to spread, so you should know how protect yourself.

E-mail Software

There are hundreds of e-mail software applications available for you to use. Some are free, some are not, and each has its advantages and disadvantages.

Some examples of e-mail software are Microsoft Outlook, Eudora, and Netscape Communicator.

For users who want to get started right away without downloading anything, Windows comes with a free e-mail application called Outlook Express, which can be configured to connect to any ISP to retrieve and send e-mail. A typical Outlook Express screen looks like the following:

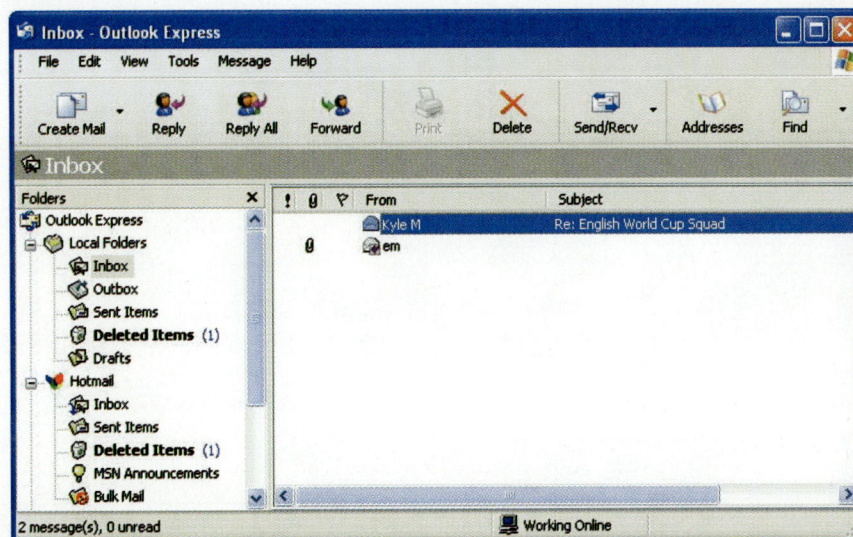

Web-based E-mail

You don't always need to be at the same computer to check your e-mail. A number of sites available online let you register for a free e-mail address and use a Web browser to send and receive messages. One of the most well-known sites like this is Hotmail, but many of the online portal sites (such as Yahoo! or Lycos — see page 65) also offer free Web-based e-mail.

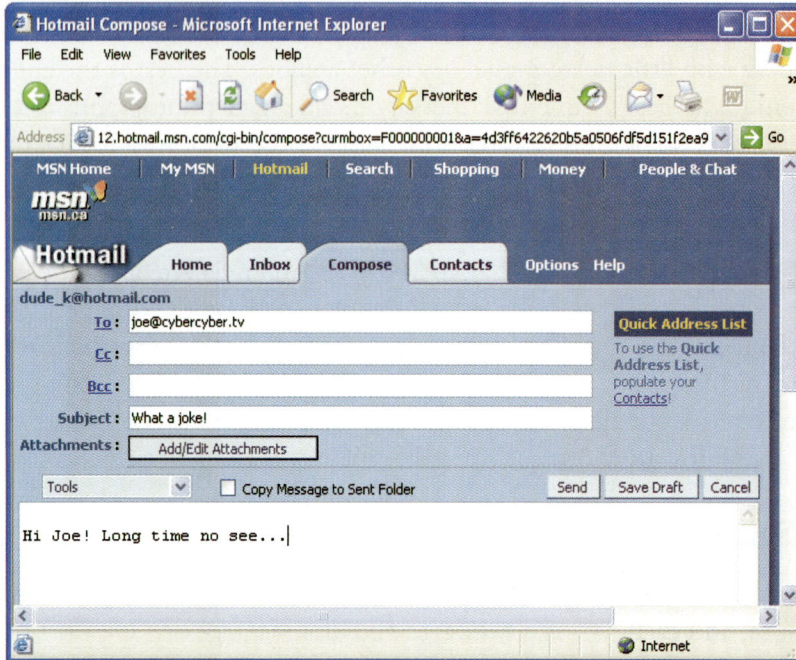

COMPUTE THIS: Web-based E-mail

Sign up for Hotmail and use it on the Web

1. Point your Web browser to www.hotmail.com, and click the **Sign up for a free e-mail account** link.
2. Fill in the profile information.
3. Scroll down, and fill in the account information.

- E-mail Address: You get to choose only the username portion. Note that the address must end with the @hotmail.com domain.
- Hotmail asks you to type the password in twice just in case you mis-type. After all, you wouldn't want to register for an account and then not be able to access it because you're not sure what to type for the password.

- The secret question and secret answer are security devices to help you in case you forget your password. If you can't remember what your password is, the Hotmail server will ask you the secret question. If you provide the correct answer, you will be allowed access to your account.

- Services: These two options list your name in the Hotmail Member Directory, and the Internet White Pages. If you really want people to be able to find you online, leave these checked. Otherwise, if you value your privacy, it might be a better idea to uncheck them.

4. Click the I Agree button when finished. You should see a message saying that the registration is complete. If not, Hotmail will indicate whether information is missing or if the address you chose is already in use. When finished, click the **Continue** button to sign on to Hotmail for the first time.

5. Scroll down in the Hotmail window that appears, and follow the link to choose the free 2 MB account.

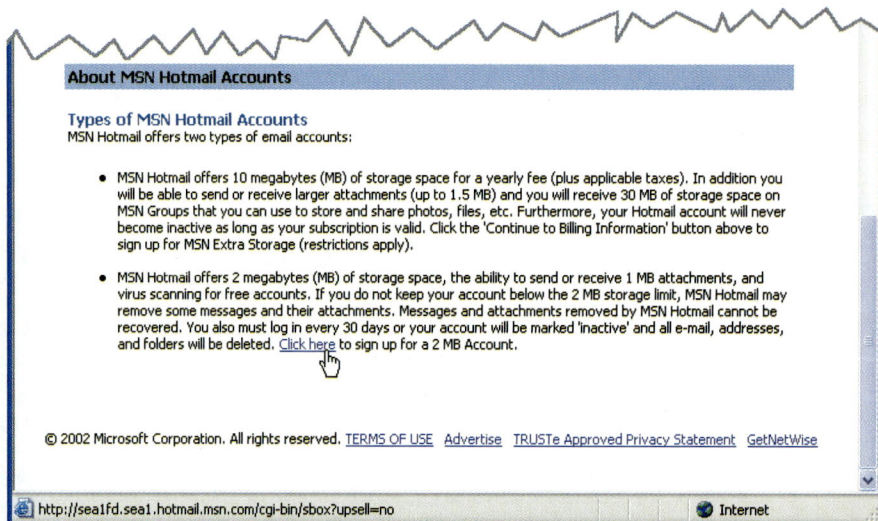

About MSN Hotmail Accounts

Types of MSN Hotmail Accounts
MSN Hotmail offers two types of email accounts:

- MSN Hotmail offers 10 megabytes (MB) of storage space for a yearly fee (plus applicable taxes). In addition you will be able to send or receive larger attachments (up to 1.5 MB) and you will receive 30 MB of storage space on MSN Groups that you can use to store and share photos, files, etc. Furthermore, your Hotmail account will never become inactive as long as your subscription is valid. Click the 'Continue to Billing Information' button above to sign up for MSN Extra Storage (restrictions apply).

- MSN Hotmail offers 2 megabytes (MB) of storage space, the ability to send or receive 1 MB attachments, and virus scanning for free accounts. If you do not keep your account below the 2 MB storage limit, MSN Hotmail may remove some messages and their attachments. Messages and attachments removed by MSN Hotmail cannot be recovered. You also must log in every 30 days or your account will be marked 'inactive' and all e-mail, addresses, and folders will be deleted. Click here to sign up for a 2 MB Account.

© 2002 Microsoft Corporation. All rights reserved. TERMS OF USE   Advertise   TRUSTe Approved Privacy Statement   GetNetWise

http://sea1fd.sea1.hotmail.msn.com/cgi-bin/sbox?upsell=no   Internet

6. The next window offers you the chance to sign up for as many newsletters as you want. These are delivered straight to your e-mail box, so if you see anything that interests you, go ahead and subscribe. You can always cancel these newsletters at a later date. Scroll down to the bottom of the page and click the **Continue** button to go on.

7. In this window, you can choose to have ads delivered directly to your e-mail box. Click anything you like, then scroll to the bottom of the page and click the **Continue to E-mail** button.

8. You are now registered with Hotmail and are looking at your Hotmail page. From here you can send e-mail messages, read e-mail messages, and start searches on the Web.

9. Be sure to click the Sign Out button (located in the upper right-hand corner of the page) when you are finished using Hotmail. Otherwise, someone else could come along and use this computer to access your Hotmail account.

Always click here to sign out of Hotmail.

Other Internet Applications

While surfing the Web and exchanging e-mail are popular activities on the Internet, there are also many other applications that can be put to good use online. Among these are instant messaging and plug-ins (smaller programs that run inside your Web browser).

Instant Messaging

You may have heard of people chatting on the Internet. **Instant messaging** is one way to do this. A short message (several lines maximum length) is instantly sent to (and received by) the other person using the program. Usually, you only send messages to people who are currently online, so you know that they have received your message. The person can then reply immediately, and in this way you can have a real-time dialogue online.

Some examples of instant messaging software are ICQ, Windows (MSN) Messenger, and AOL Instant Messenger. For the most part, each instant messaging application can only send messages to users who are connected to the Internet and using that same application, so the best way to decide which one to use is to ask around and find out what other people you know are using.

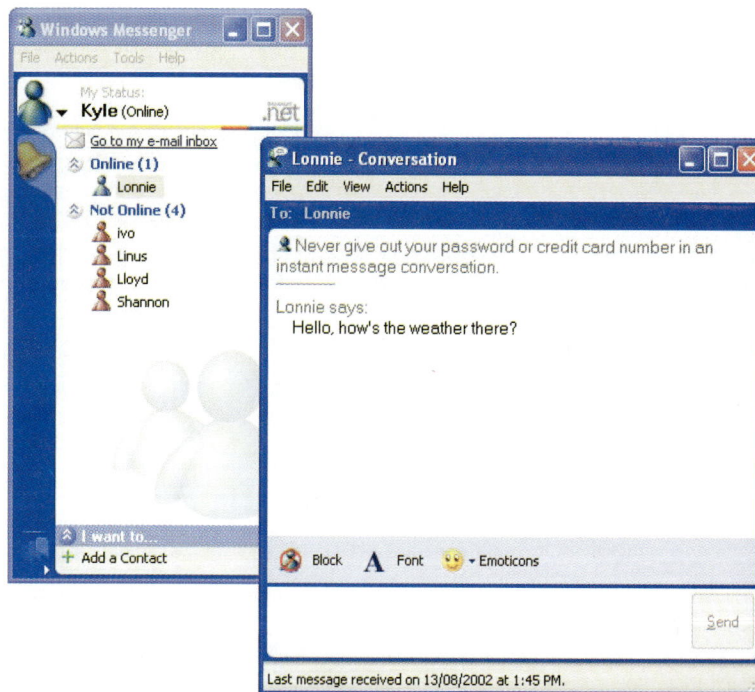

Plug-ins

A **plug-in** is a small program that "plugs into" your Web browser, allowing you to access extra features from Web sites that support that plug-in. Two of the more common ones are the Macromedia Flash and Shockwave plug-ins. The Flash plug-in is used to display Flash-format animations and graphics, while the Shockwave plug-in is used to run Shockwave games or videos.

For some good examples of how Flash can be used to create an original and effective Web site, visit some of the samples on display at the Macromedia Web site shown here:

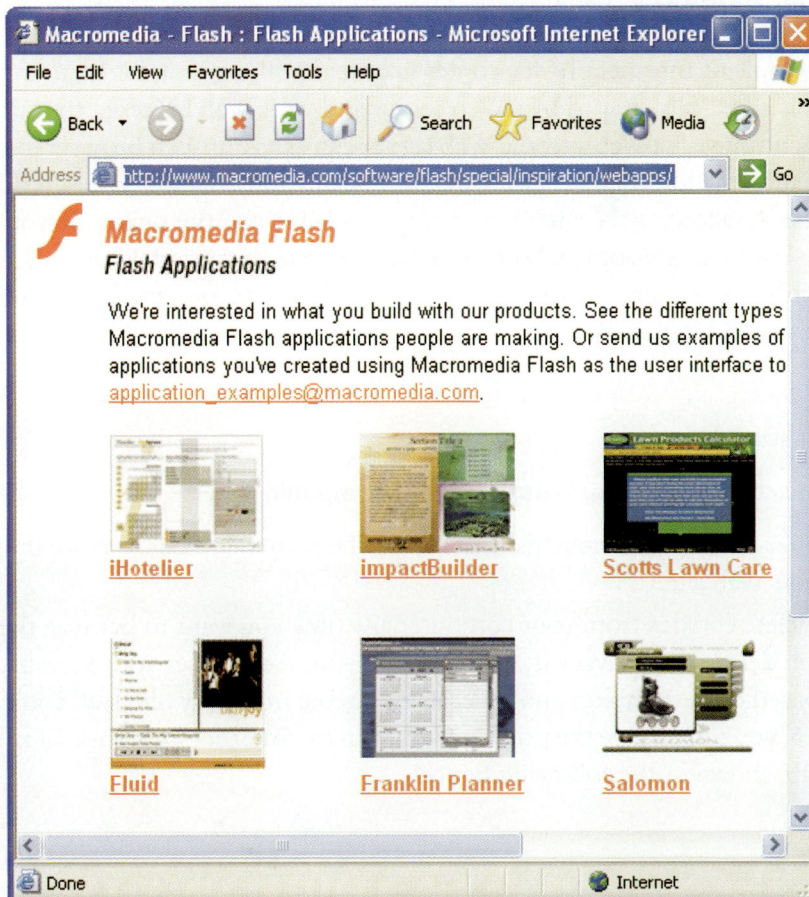

Security and Privacy

As you have already seen in the anti-virus section (page 36), security is important when you use a computer, especially online. If your Web browser is not properly configured, your computer could be left open to malicious Web sites, or a Web site could obtain personal information from you without your permission.

But in reality, the Internet isn't so grim. All current Web browsers have a number of security and privacy settings enforced by default as protection.

What Are Cookies?

When the topic of Internet privacy comes up, the first thing that comes to mind are cookies. A **cookie** is a text file, created by a Web server and your Web browser, that sits on your hard drive. When you visit a Web site, the Web server can ask your Web browser to create a cookie, and store information there. Usually, this will be any information you enter if the site asks you to register, allowing the site to customize itself for you the next time you visit. This can be useful, but there are some who believe this to be an intrusion of privacy, especially since personal information given to a site (such as your address, or a credit card number) is sometimes stored in a cookie.

Cookies

- Do not spread viruses.

- Cannot access other information on your computer.

- Cannot execute any commands themselves. They merely exist to store information for a particular Web site.

You can delete cookies from your computer any time you want to because they are only text files. If you decide that privacy is a concern for you, you can set your Web browser to block cookies based on certain sites and on certain criteria, or simply block all cookies. In Internet Explorer 6, you can change the privacy settings in the Internet Options dialog box, under the Privacy tab, shown in the following figure.

Browser Security Settings

Web browser security means protecting against anything that might be able to take advantage of your Web browser to cause fraudulent or malicious activity. This can include plug-ins, scripts (little programs run by a Web server on your computer), secure certificates (encrypted data files that are used to assure a site's authenticity), and more.

The situation isn't as bad as it sounds. Most loopholes in a browser's security are fixed by the software developers soon after they are discovered. Simply by keeping your Web browser updated (all Web browsers offer the ability to download updates form the Internet), you're protecting yourself. A Web browser's default security settings are generally sufficient. For further security (or in those rare cases where you might need to lower browser security), all Web browsers' security preferences can be customized.

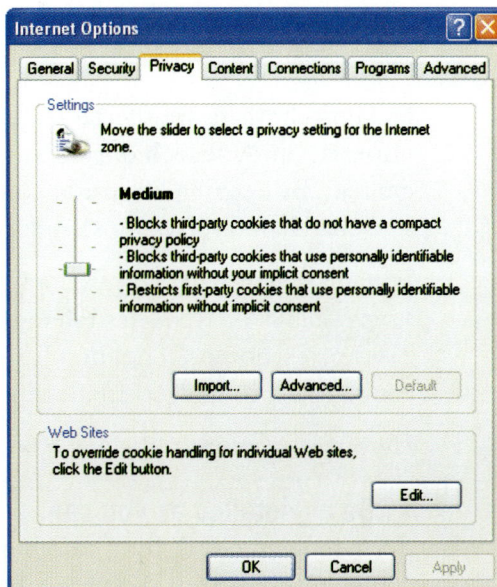

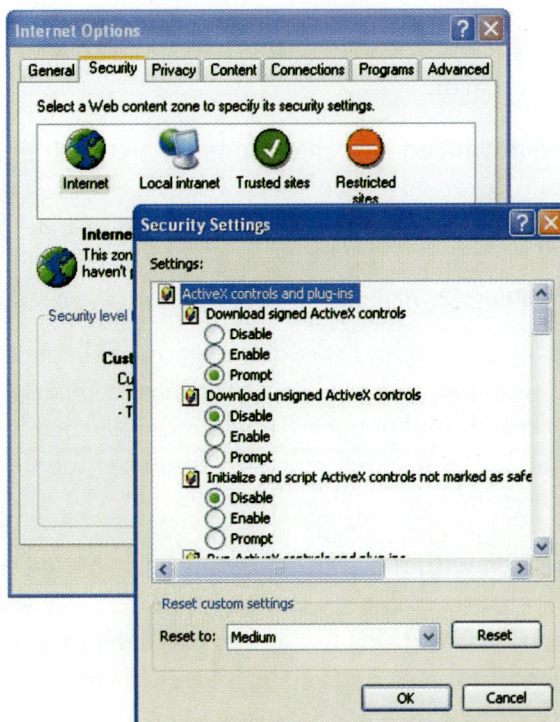

Search Tools

The Internet is a very big place and there is a lot of information out there waiting to be found — the trick is to find it.

Fortunately, there are special search engine Web sites where you can begin your search for information. A **search engine** is a Web site containing a database of Web pages and their content. By entering keywords, you tell the search engine what you're looking for and, if any sites match, it displays those sites with links to the page, along with a brief synopsis.

Finding exactly what you are looking for can be tricky, especially since most search engines have millions of Web sites referenced in their databases. A search on any given topic can easily reveal dozens, if not hundreds of results. Naturally, not every site will have exactly what you're trying to find, so conducting a successful search on the Internet can be challenging.

Here are seven tips to help you conduct a successful Internet search:

■ **Be as detailed as you can.**

Typing in "used car" for a search is going to get you a lot of results, most of which will be completely irrelevant. You probably won't want to know that a car is for sale in Gnome, Alaska, unless of course you're in Alaska.

Include as many keywords as you can to narrow down the search. "Used cars for sale St. Cloud Minnesota GM" will probably turn up results in your area (if you live near Minneapolis) for the type of car you're seeking, and you'll have to sort through fewer links before finding what you want.

■ **Learn to use the advanced search options on a search engine.**

Many search engines offer an advanced search feature, either by using Boolean logic operators (And, Not, Or, and so on.), or by using a series of pull-down menus to specify the conditions of the search. Using advanced search options will help narrow down the results returned by the search engine, making it easier to locate the results you need.

For example, a search for "puppies for adoption german shepherd" will return results that contain puppies for adoption, and will likely contain references to German Shepherd puppies. However, a search for "puppies for adoption German Shepherd NOT labrador" will not return results that contain references to Labrador puppies, reducing the number of irrelevant results to sort through.

■ **Try the same search with different combinations of key words.**

If you still can't find what you want, try choosing different key words. Instead of searching for "resorts Caribbean," try searching for "hotels bars cabins Caribbean." Not everyone uses the same words to describe things, and varying the search around the same theme can return vastly different results.

■ **Consider the source of the site.**

Remember, just because you read it on the Internet, doesn't mean it's true. This is especially true when you're researching information. Pay close attention to who is posting this information (which organization or individual). Read carefully and look for sources and references. For example, a recognized medical university's Web site should have more valid medical information than the online journal entry of someone who claims to be a plastic surgeon.

■ **Use more than one search engine.**

Every search engine uses different methods to find, sort, and categorize its database of Web sites. If you can't find what you want on one search engine, don't just stop there, try others. A search on three or more search engines will give you a much more complete picture of what is "out there" on the Internet.

■ **Bookmark as many search sites as you can.**

The more often you search on the Internet, the more search engines you will come across. Don't rely on your memory to find that new search engine again the next time your favorite search engine fails to find what you want. Bookmark it immediately, even if you won't use it right away. As mentioned in the previous tip, there is no such things as using too many search engines.

A bookmark is a link you can create directly to a specific Web page, so that you can visit it at any time by going directly to that page. Bookmark, in fact, is only the name given to this kind of link inside Netscape. If you are using Internet Explorer, these links are called Favorites. Whatever the name, they serve exactly the same purpose: to mark sites that you would like to visit again.

■ **Find the search site that best accommodates your type of search.**

After using several different search engines for a while, you will begin to notice that certain engines work better for finding certain subjects. Make note of these, and remember to use them again the next time you carry out a similar search.

Also, there are some specialized search engines on the Internet. Should you run across any of these, definitely bookmark them for future reference, because one search on a specialized search engine can be worth ten searches of the general type.

COMPUTE THIS: Sample Search Engines

The following is a far-from-exhaustive list of useful search engines on the World Wide Web:

Search Engines

Search Engines: These are your bread-and-butter search engines.

Google:	www.google.ca
AltaVista:	www.altavista.com
All the Web:	www.alltheweb.com

Meta Search Engines: This type of search engine runs your search for you on several different search engines at a time, instead of maintaining its own database. When it has a certain number of results, it displays the links for you.

Ixquick:	www.ixquick.com
Kartoo:	www.kartoo.com
Mamma:	www.mamma.com

Specialized Search Engines: Certain search engines seek out only specific types of Web sites. This is good for in-depth searches on a subject the search site specializes in.

TripAdvisor:	www.tripadvisor.com	Travel information
BioView:	www.bioview.com	Biological science information
RocketNews:	www.rocketnews.com	Recent news items

Common Portals

A **portal** on the Internet is meant to be a launching point for your browsing online. It offers as many services and conveniences as possible, to encourage you to use the site often. From an Internet portal, you can check news, search the Web, check e-mail, and any other combination of online activities. Most Web portals have some sort of theme, and the bulk of the services revolve around that theme.

Search Portals

- Yahoo! is one of the most well-known portals. From Yahoo!, you can search the Web, shop, chat, check e-mail, or build a Web site. (Yahoo! started as a search engine.) www.yahoo.com

- Lycos is another search engine-turned-Web-portal. Lycos also offers services for just about everything you could look for on the Web. www.lycos.com

Buy/Trade/Sell

- Ebay hosts auction sales from around the world, as well as certain types of online shopping. If you are looking for bargains or interesting items for sales, this can be one of the best starting points on the Web. www.ebay.com

News Portals

- BBC — From this site visitors can search the Web, read international news, visit links to BBC media channels, and check the weather. This site is mainly tailored to visitors from the United Kingdom. www.bbc.co.uk

- New York Times — This site's main purpose is to convey news from the New York Times newspaper, but it also provides links to job searching, real estate listings, and stock quotes. This site is mainly tailored for American visitors. www.nytimes.com